EUTHANASIA
ALL THAT MATTERS

EUTHANASIA

Richard Huxtable

ALL THAT MATTERS

ALL THAT MATTERS

First published in Great Britain in 2013 by Hodder & Stoughton. An Hachette UK company.

First published in US in 2013 by The McGraw-Hill Companies, Inc.

This edition published 2013

Copyright © Richard Huxtable 2013

The right of Richard Huxtable to be identified as the Author of the Work has been asserted by him in accordance with the Copyright, Designs and Patents Act 1988.

Database right Hodder & Stoughton (makers)

British Library Cataloguing in Publication Data: a catalogue record for this title is available from the British Library.

Library of Congress Catalog Card Number: on file.

10 9 8 7 6 5 4 3 2 1

The publisher has used its best endeavours to ensure that any website addresses referred to in this book are correct and active at the time of going to press. However, the publisher and the author have no responsibility for the websites and can make no guarantee that a site will remain live or that the content will remain relevant, decent or appropriate.

The publisher has made every effort to mark as such all words which it believes to be trademarks. The publisher should also like to make it clear that the presence of a word in the book, whether marked or unmarked, in no way affects its legal status as a trademark.

Every reasonable effort has been made by the publisher to trace the copyright holders of material in this book. Any errors or omissions should be notified in writing to the publisher, who will endeavour to rectify the situation for any reprints and future editions.

Typeset by Cenveo® Publisher Services.

Printed and bound in Great Britain by CPI Group (UK) Ltd, Croydon CR0 4YY.

Hodder & Stoughton policy is to use papers that are natural, renewable and recyclable products and made from wood grown in sustainable forests. The logging and manufacturing processes are expected to conform to the environmental regulations of the country of origin.

Hodder & Stoughton Ltd

338 Euston Road

London NW1 3BH

www.hodder.co.uk

Also available in ebook

For Mum and Dad – with love and thanks

Contents

1

Dying matters

'The miracles of modern medicine may save many, but they can condemn patients to poor-quality lives of incapacity and dependence.'

ALL THAT MATTERS

Despite his long experience, Abrenuncio felt pity for the rabies victim. 'The human body is not made to endure all the years that one may live,' he said. The Marquis did not miss a word of his exhaustive and colourful discourse, and spoke only when the doctor had nothing more to say.

'What can be done for that poor man?' he asked.

'Kill him,' said Abrenuncio.

The Marquis looked at him, appalled.

'At least that is what we would do if we were good Christians,' the impassive doctor continued. 'And never fear, Señor: there are more good Christians than one supposes.' (García Márquez 1996: 19)

Rabies is less likely nowadays to present the predicament pondered by the characters in Gabriel García Márquez's novel, which is set in the eighteenth century. But the central dilemma lingers, whether one is atheist, agnostic, Christian or committed to some other faith: Can it be right to end a life of suffering?

Scan the international media on any given day and the question is often being asked. The miracles of modern medicine may save many, but they can condemn patients to poor-quality lives of incapacity and dependence. 'Developing' countries confront the increasing incidence of AIDS, while their 'developed' neighbours strive to provide for ageing populations. Increasingly, one hears pleas not only of 'Let me die' but also 'Help me to die'. The story of Anna amply illustrates many of the areas of difficulty.

Anna was a schoolteacher who lived in New Zealand with her husband and their three young children. Always an active person, Anna had loved hiking and amateur dramatics, and she was regarded as a very talented singer. However, life changed dramatically following a serious road accident that left Anna tetraplegic. Largely paralysed, Anna also suffered considerable pain, which powerful painkillers sought to control.

Scarcely able to move and incapable of undertaking the activities she so valued, Anna did not recognize this existence as her life – and certainly not as a life worth living. She made it clear to her doctors and carers that, should the need arise, she would not want them to make efforts to resuscitate her. However, when her usual carers were away, Anna suffered breathing difficulties and a different team intervened and resuscitated her. Anna was then placed on a ventilator, where it seemed she would need to remain.

Anna insisted that the machine be removed. She knew full well that, without the ventilator, she would be likely to die. The hospital's lawyers and ethics committee saw no legal or ethical barrier to granting Anna's request. Preparations were therefore made to withdraw the treatment: the medical team set up a device that enabled Anna herself to switch off the machine, using the little movement she had left in her fingers. With her family present, Anna pressed the button. The doctors then administered drugs to alleviate any respiratory distress that Anna might endure and she slipped into unconsciousness.

Soon afterwards, Anna awoke and asked angrily, 'Why am I still here?' She appeared to be one of the few patients in her specific situation whose body retained some ability to breathe unaided. The doctors confronted a fresh dilemma: Should they reinstate the machine if Anna again experienced breathing difficulties? In the event, they elected to give Anna more medication. She once more slipped into unconsciousness. Some hours later her breathing ceased and Anna died (Campbell 1998: 83–4).

▶ When *I* use a word...

'When I use a word,' Humpty Dumpty said, in rather a scornful tone,' it means just what I choose it to mean – neither more or less.' 'The question is,' said Alice, 'whether you can make words mean so many different things.' (Carroll (1871) 1982: 184)

▲ Lewis Carroll's Humpty Dumpty character in *Alice through the Looking Glass* suggests that words can have different meanings for different people.

In order best to understand Anna's story, we should take a moment to consider the different terms that are used in current debates about ending life.

Euthanasia (from the Greek *eu* and *thanatos*) translates as 'good death'. But this, of course, begs the moral question about whether death can be 'good'. Better, these days, to think of euthanasia as the intentional ending of a life of suffering, usually by a doctor. *Assisted dying* conveys the same concept (although it tends to be reserved for euthanasia on request). Where the assistant is not a doctor but is instead a loved one, then *mercy killing* is the term that tends to be used.

A distinction might then be drawn between *active* and *passive* euthanasia. Giving a lethal injection would count as 'active', while some would say that denying (or even removing) life-supporting treatment amounts to 'passive' euthanasia.

Another distinction refers to the person subjected to euthanasia, and specifically his or her ability to agree to it. Where he or she makes the relevant request, this will be *voluntary*; where he or she does not (and perhaps even objects outright), then this will be *involuntary*; and where he or she lacks the ability to do either (say, because they are a baby or are comatose), this will be *non-voluntary*.

Finally (for now), there is *assisted suicide*, in which the final, fatal act is performed by the suffering individual, such as when they consume the pills provided by an assistant. The assistant may be a doctor, as in *physician-assisted suicide*.

None of these concepts is straightforward. What counts as 'intending' to end life? Indeed, what counts as 'life' – and as 'death'? Isn't involuntary euthanasia just murder? And why is pulling out a tube 'passive'? The terms are also inevitably value-laden: the way that someone like Humpty Dumpty seeks to use words can tell us much about their moral perspective on a situation like Anna's. Did her story involve passive euthanasia? Active euthanasia? Something else entirely? We will return to these questions – and these concepts – throughout this book. Let us start by considering some of the underlying moral matters, and particularly those which concern one of philosophy's enduring questions: What is the value of human life?

▶ Judging the value of life

Anna's story invites us to consider three prominent positions on the value of life. First, there is the idea that life has *intrinsic* value. On this view, human life is so worth while that it should not intentionally be brought to a premature end – either by (positive) action, like a lethal injection, or by (negative) omission, such as withholding nutrition. The idea will be well known to the Christians to whom Abrenuncio (at the start of this chapter) referred, since it conveys the sanctity of human life, which is also recognized in many other faiths. But one need not believe in any deity to sign up to the central idea. Nowadays one often hears appeals to human rights, perhaps the most fundamental of which is the right to life.

According to scholars like John Keown (2002), even an unwilling patient like Anna has an intrinsically valuable life, which should be protected and preserved. Of course, Anna disagreed. She sought to reject the existence she faced following the accident. Judging by their behaviour, her doctors sympathized and might even have shared her view. Keown, however, would argue against any deliberate attempt to shorten life, even when the life has a poor quality and is unwanted by the person herself.

Keown's position on the value of life seems to see life as a biological matter: being alive matters. So long as the person has not been declared brainstem dead, then even the permanently unconscious life warrants the same protection as that afforded to the able-bodied and agile-minded. But there are those who complain that this offers an impoverished account of the value of human life. Instead, they argue, life has only *instrumental* value.

According to this view, life is only a *vehicle* to the things that really make it worth living: dinner with family and friends, travel, or, for Anna, hiking and amateur dramatics. When the vehicle can no longer get us to where we want to go, so the argument runs, then it may be time to trade it in. Put more explicitly, sometimes a life may be so blighted by suffering that it may be better for it to be brought to an early end.

Philosophers like Peter Singer and John Harris believe that this sort of argument can apply to some critically ill infants and permanently unconscious adults, for whom killing might be considered a kindness (Singer 1993; Harris 1985). Of course, killing might also be a kindness for some fully conscious, but suffering, adults. But while we might have to rely on the opinions of parents, doctors or judges when deciding for a suffering baby, such adults will be able to tell us their own views on this issue. Here, a third approach to the value of life emerges, which points to its *self-determined* value.

Advocates of the self-determined value of life see decisions about how one exits life as a matter for the individual in question. 'Whose life is it anyway?' as Brian Clark's play so powerfully puts it (Clark 1984). Associated with this perspective are many ideas that we tend to hold in high regard in the modern health-care setting: choice, informed consent, privacy and the right to refuse unwanted treatment.

Underpinning all of these ideas is the concept of autonomy, from the Greek *auto* (self) and *nomos* (rule). When autonomy is our guide, it is argued, even our very concept of 'life' should shift, from a fixation on the biological and the body, to concerns with the (auto)biographical and thus the mind. So, says Ronald Dworkin (1993: 217), making someone like Anna endure an unwanted and unrecognized 'life' is 'a devastating, odious form of tyranny'.

▶ Judging the judgements

What are we to make of these competing perspectives on the value of life? Each seems to tell us something important – about our obligations to preserve life, eradicate suffering, and honour choices. Each also commands a great deal of support. But can we conclude that any one is decisively better than its rivals?

One way of trying to decide might be to look beneath the different versions of the value of life, to see how their defenders arrived at their chosen view. Philosophers committed to very different moral theories can undoubtedly arrive at the same place. But some of the arguments we just surveyed seem to owe more to one particular way of thinking about 'the right' or 'the good'.

So we see, in the intrinsic value of life, a focus on duties, rights and intentions. These ideas connect with *deontological* theories, from the Greek *deon* (duty). Such theories judge the morality of an action in terms of that action's adherence to some rule or rules. The German philosopher Immanuel Kant (1724–1804) emphasized the 'good will'. He offered various versions of what he called the 'categorical imperative', the most famous of which are: 'Act only according to that maxim (or principle) by which you can also will that it would become a universal law' and 'Act in such a way that you always treat humanity, whether in your own person or in the person of any other, never simply as a means, but always at the same time as an end' (Kant (1785) 1991). Kant therefore asks us to consider what the world would look like if everyone did as we did, and he asks us to treat people as worthy of respect. These ideas seem to stress the intrinsic worth of humans – an idea clearly echoed in the first account of the value of life.

Of course, not everyone shares Kant's fixation on duties. Consequentialists, as the name implies, see morality as concerned with the consequences or outcomes of one's actions. Utilitarians take this approach. The English philosopher Jeremy Bentham (1748–1832) is closely associated with this way of thinking (Warnock (ed.) 1962). His ideas were developed by his student John Stuart Mill (1806–73), who argued that one must act to produce the greatest happiness for the greatest number (Warnock (ed.) 1962). Modern utilitarians, however, tend to talk of maximizing welfare (not merely pleasure). Hence we see, in Peter Singer's work, welfare-driven arguments to the effect that the removal of suffering – even through killing – can be an appropriate outcome for some people.

Yet, like Mill, who was also concerned with individual liberty, Singer still wants people's preferences to be given due respect. One need not be a consequentialist to think this: deontologists and feminist philosophers, for example, will say similar things. So, too, might those who believe that morality is not entirely tethered to duties and outcomes and thus to action. Virtue ethicists, for example, tend to focus on character. For the ancient Greek philosopher Aristotle (384–322 BCE), cultivating the virtues can lead to *eudaimonia* (flourishing), which is the proper goal of human life (Aristotle [350 BCE] 2009). Contemporary virtue ethicists who write about death and dying, such as Liezl van Zyl, therefore suggest that our concern with autonomy is better expressed in terms of a virtue like 'respectfulness' (Van Zyl 2000).

Perhaps one of these accounts of moral theory will seem more persuasive than the others, and will help in determining which account of the value of life should be our guide. But, perhaps instead, we have simply moved the goal posts. For the same question remains, which has now become: Which of these theories looks strongest?

There are many things we might look for when deciding on moral matters. At a minimum, we need our moral guidance (whatever it might say) to be clear, consistent and capable of being applied in the real world in which we live. But we also need it to be capable of surviving scrutiny: we need the arguments to work and to withstand even the strongest counter-arguments. Here Lewis Carroll's Alice might once more help us to organize our thoughts.

Alice's exchange with Humpty Dumpty invited us to consider what words might mean, and how they might be used (or, perhaps, misused). This provides one way of scrutinizing moral arguments: What concepts are involved, and what can and should they be taken to mean?

A second way is provided by Tweedledee: '...if it was so, it might be; and if it were so, it would be; but as it isn't, it ain't. That's logic' (Carroll 1982: 157). So, we might ask, what is the logic of the argument being defended? Where might it take us? What does it presuppose or entail?

Thirdly, we have a very telling exchange between Alice and a mouse:

> 'Oh, I beg your pardon!' cried Alice hastily, afraid that she had hurt the poor animal's feelings. 'I quite forgot you didn't like cats.' 'Not like cats!' cried the Mouse, in a shrill, passionate voice. 'Would you like cats if you were me?' (Carroll (1871) 1982: 29)

Here we might ask: What sort of reception to the argument being advanced could we expect? How appealing is it likely to be, in the real world?

As we proceed through this book, it will be worth bearing in mind Alice's lessons, and considering the questions of meaning, scope and appeal that will inevitably arise as we delve into the moral dimensions of end-of-life decision-making. As we debate the issues, we are likely to differ in our conclusions about which of the versions of the value of life is most persuasive. What remains important, however, is that we are open to the debate. In the words of the Dying Matters coalition in the UK, 'dying matters – let's talk about it' (www.dyingmatters.org). So let us get talking by considering, in more depth, the idea that life has intrinsic value.

2

Drawing lines

'Quality-of-life judgements are essentially relative, either to some previously enjoyed quality of life or to the perceived quality of others' lives. Who is to make such judgements?'

ALL THAT MATTERS

> 'We hold these truths to be self-evident, that all
> men are created equal, that they are endowed by
> their Creator with certain unalienable Rights, that
> among these are Life, Liberty, and the Pursuit of
> Happiness.'

The opening sentence of the United States Declaration of Independence, written by Thomas Jefferson in 1776, captures something of the idea that life has intrinsic value. The notion of equality is crucial here: despite the reference to 'men' in the Declaration, the fundamental right to life accrues regardless of (say) gender, ethnicity or sexuality. But the corresponding duty to protect life is not boundless. Even supporters of the sanctity of life recognize that lines may be drawn.

In that case: Gracie and Rosie

In 2000 Michaelangelo and Rina Attard left their Maltese home for Manchester, England. The couple sought expert advice at St Mary's Hospital, as they were expecting conjoined twins.

The twins were born in October by caesarean section. Gracie and Rosie were 'ischiopagus tetrapus' conjoined twins: they each had their own arms and legs, but they were joined at the pelvis, with a fused spine. Each girl had her own vital organs, although they shared a liver and bladder and also a circulatory system, as they were joined at the main artery. But Rosie's heart and lungs were malformed and did not function. Gracie's heart and lungs were therefore doing all of the work for both girls, in pumping oxygenated blood throughout their shared body.

The doctors believed that, if Rosie and Gracie were to remain joined, Gracie's heart would fail within a matter of months and both girls would die. They thought Rosie would not have survived without her sister; Gracie, however, could be expected to lead a relatively 'normal' life – but only if she was separated from her dependent sibling. Yet, the separation operation would cause Rosie's death. Michaelangelo and Rina, devout Roman Catholics, could not consent: they saw the girls as equal, and could not agree to kill one, even to save the other.

The hospital sought the High Court's guidance. Here the girls' identities were protected (Gracie becoming Jodie, Rosie becoming Mary), although the parents later chose to go public. Mr Justice Johnson saw Rosie's dependence on Gracie as similar to other patients' reliance on life-prolonging treatment, such as might be provided by tubes and machines. The separation operation was like the 'withdrawal' of treatment: it was, he reasoned, in the 'best interests' of Rosie, who could not survive alone, to have this burden removed.

A superior court, the Court of Appeal, agreed with this result but not the reasoning. On balance, said the judges, separation would indeed be in the 'best interests' of Gracie. One of the judges, Lord Justice Walker, was even prepared to say that this would also be in Rosie's 'best interests', because, he said, separation would respect her right to 'a whole body'. But this would clearly involve a 'positive' action, quite distinct from any removal of treatment. Although this would usually amount to murder, these doctors could plead a defence: their action was either justified as 'necessary' in order to save Gracie or it otherwise amounted to a sort of 'self-defence' of her, with (said the judges) the doctors acting on Gracie's likely protest: 'Stop it ... you're killing me.'

On 6 November 2000, the surgeons thus embarked on a 20-hour operation, with two of them holding the scalpel when it made the final cut. As expected, Rosie died; Gracie, meanwhile, recovered well, and she returned with her parents to Malta to live life as a 'singleton' (*Re A* (2000); Boseley 2002).

▲ 'Jodie and Mary': To separate or not to separate?

In reaching their decision, the senior judges sought to apply the sanctity of human life principle. In doing so, they mentioned many related principles, which help draw lines between what one should and should not do when trying to treat life as sacred. Fundamentally, one should not intentionally bring life to a premature end. This invites a question: What counts as 'life' here?

▶ Life and everything in between

'What is this creature in the eyes of the law?' asked Lord Justice Brooke of Gracie and Rosie. The law answered that there were two people, but philosophers have long argued about what it is that makes a 'person', and particularly one meriting special moral concern.

Some of those committed to the intrinsic value of life believe that life begins at conception. For them, Gracie and Rosie will have had intrinsic worth from this point on. Some advocates of the instrumental value of life, however, insist that personhood consists in the acquisition and retention of certain capacities, like the ability to reason or value one's existence. Where the mind is absent, they say, so, too, is the person: without the ghost within, our bodies are merely machines. For them, neither Gracie nor Rosie would necessarily have a right to life as such (although they may have some interests), since their infancy prevented them from possessing the characteristics necessary for full personhood.

Others occupy the middle ground, as they argue that moral worth develops between conception and 'personhood'. Such 'gradualists' point to the embryo's potential for development into tomorrow's autonomous adult. There may be crucial stages in this development, such as the appearance of the 'primitive streak' in the embryo, at which point an individual apparently begins to develop. There are also the very visible variations of childhood, like first steps and first words. Gradualist positions reflect these changes by attaching growing moral worth to the developing embryo or infant. Many legal systems take this approach, permitting the termination of pregnancy or embryo research early on, but affording more protection to the growing embryo and certainly more to the child once born.

Various analogies have been advanced to explore these different views. Judith Jarvis Thomson, for example, compares pregnancy to someone (let's say me) being hooked up to a famous violinist without their prior permission. The violinist now needs my body's support for nine months, or else he will die (Thomson 1971). Thomson suggests I may say that this situation is unjust and should be stopped (even if it kills the violinist). Implicit in her account seems to be the idea that this is my body and these are my organs. But can we say the same of Rosie and Gracie? Given that they were conjoined, can we be sure that Gracie 'owned' the stronger organs?

▶ Intending, foreseeing, acting, omitting

Even if we think the stronger organs are Gracie's, Rosie could still complain that she is being sacrificed. This looks like a problem in terms of the intrinsic value of her life. One way out of this problem involves focusing on the doctors' aims. Need we say that they 'intended' to kill Rosie?

The doctrine of double effect holds that there is a difference between intending and (merely) foreseeing a 'bad' outcome like death. Recognizing the intrinsic value of life involves avoiding the former. Foreseen 'bad' effects may still be allowed, provided that four conditions are met:

1 The act itself is good, or at least neutral;

2 The good effect is not obtained by means of the bad one;

3 The bad effect is not intended, but only foreseen and permitted; and

4 There is a proportionately strong reason for permitting the bad effect.

We will revisit this principle in Chapter 7. When considering the conjoined twins, however, it presents us with a problem: however 'good' separation might look for Gracie, it seems it can be achieved only in a manner that ends Rosie's life. It therefore appears that the 'good' effect can only result from the 'bad' one.

Is there more merit in Mr Justice Johnson's approach, in which we see separation as akin to the removal of treatment from Rosie? The distinction between actions and omissions is also relied on by advocates of the intrinsic value of life. So, they say, we can never *aim* at ending life – whether by action or omission – but some omissions *can* be allowed, when, for example, treatment appears 'futile' or will involve disproportionate burdens for the individual, which outweigh any benefits they might expect.

We will also revisit these ideas, in Chapter 6. For now, we need only note the difficulty – recognized by Johnson's senior colleagues – in applying these ideas to Gracie and Rosie. Critics have queried what counts as an 'omission': Withholding something seems to do so, but what about withdrawing a tube, which might require a physical act for its removal? This complaint seems well founded here: surgically cutting the twins apart certainly looks some considerable distance from (for example) no longer supplying nutrients down a feeding tube.

▶ Judging Rosie and Gracie

The judges seem to have exhausted their avenues for upholding the intrinsic value of Rosie's life. Although they still seemed to think they were doing so, a different ethic seems to be at work in the judges' reasoning. Even the proclaimed self-defence of Gracie looks shaky: Why assume that a sister would protest like this? And why could Rosie not equally claim that, in allowing separation to occur, it was she who was being killed by being left to die?

Lord Justice Brooke's reference to the 'creature' before the court seems to indicate the real approach being taken. Here was a being qualitatively distinct from many other humans. And Rosie, the weaker sibling, also differed from her stronger sister. Weakness – and other considerations associated with the 'quality' of life, such as the 'happiness' to which the Declaration of Independence referred – come to the fore when we see life in *instrumental*, rather than intrinsic, terms. And it seems most likely that it was this, the instrumental value of life, with which the judges were concerned.

We saw, in Chapter 1, how considerations of the instrumental value of life can be tied to consequentialist accounts of morality, according to which outcomes count, rather than observance of duties like the duty not to kill. Notice the message sent by the judges' decision: one life saved is better than two lives lost. The choice of which life to save is made by comparing the potential quality of each girl's life. In the words of Lord Justice Ward, Gracie could be expected to live a 'normal' life – but only when freed of her 'parasitic' sister. Rosie, meanwhile, was already 'designated for death', given her 'hopeless' situation. According to this logic, Rosie must therefore be sacrificed for the good of her sister.

How far could or should this logic extend? Alice Domurat Dreger has written persuasively that we should not be too quick to judge conjoined lives as poor (Dreger 2004). The famous 'Siamese twins' Chang and Eng Bunker (1811–74) may have spent periods touring as a public exhibit, but they also ran a business and each married and fathered children. Although separation is possible for many such twins today, many also value their unity. And, says Dreger, we should not assume that 'singletons' are so different: we should not be blinded to the connections we share by perceptions of individuality and normality.

A fixation on normality might even be dangerous. Quality-of-life judgements are essentially relative, either to some previously enjoyed quality of life or to the perceived quality of others' lives. Who is to make such judgements? And when are we to say that an existence is so impoverished that it should be brought to an end? We will consider further, in Chapter 9, the idea of 'slippery slopes', according to which a step in a particular, desired direction might take us into less desirable territory, which suggests that we should avoid taking the first step. Suffice to say here that we should bear in mind how judgements about the apparent quality of even the most compromised existence can encourage (either in principle or in practice) other such judgements – maybe even about the quality of our own lives.

For their part, the judges in Rosie and Gracie's case felt that they could put the brakes on any slide down a slippery slope. They claimed that their decision only applied here, for these sisters. But the law does not work like this, as the judges were soon forced to recognize. Many legal systems operate a system of precedent, according to which previous rulings are available for application in similar later cases.

So it was that, only months later, a judge in Australia applied the Attard ruling in a case concerning Bethany and Alyssa Nolan, who were joined at the head (*State of Qld v Alyssa Nolan & Anor* (2001)). Bethany, the weaker twin, had reached a point where her death was expected to occur within a matter of hours. Considering Australian law, the judge recognized the doctors' conflicting duties to the twins. Using the English ruling, he concluded that this conflict could be resolved by offering Alyssa the chance of life, through separation.

Clearly, then, judges have to appreciate that their rulings can be made to apply to people in the future – not only to those people before them in court at a particular time. It seems reasonable to suppose that our own judgements – about moral matters – might function in similar ways. We should bear this in mind as we continue to work through the different dilemmas that can arise at the end of life.

In these first two chapters we have covered much ground, some of which we will revisit. The topics we will cover are not easy. Although conjoined twins are rare, sometimes the issues will be familiar to many. We will all confront the loss of loved ones. But maybe, if we dismantle some of the taboos that surround death, we can (to quote 1 Corinthians) rob death of some of its cruel 'sting'. One way of doing so may simply be to talk about death and dying; another might be to plan, such as by preparing a 'bucket list' of things we wish to do before we die. And sometimes plans might be made for the end of our days: not just wills, but 'living wills', which cover the treatment we want – and do not want – at the end.

Such statements seek to express our autonomous wishes. But what does autonomy mean? And why and when might we have a right, autonomously, to refuse treatment that could otherwise keep us alive? It is to these questions we turn next.

3

Letting go

'...we should be free to be ourselves, living our lives – and organizing our deaths – in the ways we see fit. But how far should this freedom extend?'

ALL THAT MATTERS

Be yourself; everyone else is already taken.

Oscar Wilde's characteristic wit neatly conveys the idea at the heart of the self-determined value of life: we should be free to be ourselves, living our lives – and organizing our deaths – in the ways we see fit. But how far should this freedom extend? And when might a decision properly be described as 'ours'?

Such questions have arisen for patients throughout the world, from Anna in New Zealand to Piergiorgio Welby, a patient in Italy who publicly argued for a 'right to die' (Fisher 2006). The essence of their pleas is clear: 'Let me go.' Yet letting go is not always easy, as the story of 'Ms B', which unfolded in an English courtroom, demonstrates.

In that case: 'Ms B'

Ms B was born in Jamaica but she moved to the UK when she was aged eight. Overcoming a difficult childhood, she qualified as a social worker, rising to become head of the hospital department in which she worked. Unfortunately, her career abruptly ended when, in February 2001, a blood vessel burst in her neck, leaving her tetraplegic and thus paralysed from the neck down.

After being admitted to hospital, Ms B experienced difficulty in breathing, so she was placed on a ventilator. Within a month she began to object to this unwanted machine. The team caring for Ms B sought outside help in assessing her 'capacity' to make this decision. Three psychiatrists assessed the patient, differing in their conclusions. However, by August, Ms B's capacity to decide was confirmed. The hospital staff thereafter treated Ms B as capable of making her own decisions in every respect – except in the one area that she judged to be crucial, because they did not withdraw the life-sustaining treatment.

The team caring for Ms B had established a close bond with her. Some of its members also felt that they could not, in good conscience, comply with what they saw as her wish to die. A compromise was proposed: a 'one-way weaning programme' by which Ms B's reliance on the machine would be reduced. But Ms B remained steadfast: she wanted the ventilator to be withdrawn completely. Yet still the treatment continued.

Ms B was sufficiently aggrieved by January 2002 that she brought legal proceedings against the hospital, arguing that continued treatment amounted to 'trespass to her person'. A leading judge, Dame Elizabeth Butler-Sloss, agreed with Ms B. The principles of law relating to 'mental capacity' were said to be 'clear'. A competent patient is one who can understand and retain information relevant to the decision, believes this information, and can use it to arrive at a decision. A patient who has such capacity has the right to refuse treatment – even if this treatment was sustaining their life – whether their decision was rational or irrational, or even if no reasons were given.

The judge confirmed that Ms B was indeed a competent patient, who therefore had the right to decide. For failing to honour this right, the hospital owed Ms B compensation. As a former employee of the NHS (National Health Service), Ms B did not wish to deprive the service of much-needed funds, so she accepted a nominal amount of £100, to mark the harm done to her.

However, the judge did not overlook the concerns of the clinicians: in recognition of their right not to be involved in procedures to which they conscientiously objected, Ms B was moved to a different hospital, where doctors were willing to respect her wishes. Although the judge hoped that Ms B would reconsider her decision, she remained firm. Treatment was indeed withdrawn and Ms B died on 24 April 2002 (*Re B* (2002); BBC News 2002; Huxtable 2002).

▲ An artist's impression of Ms B giving evidence from her hospital bed

▶ Those who trespass against us?

Many legal systems adopt the line taken in English law (which generally covers both England and Wales), according to which our bodies are inviolable – unless an all-important consent is given. Consent thus underpins the permission granted to surgeons who seek to perform operations, physiotherapists who might be involved in physical manipulation, and countless more who make contact with the bodies of others.

As we see in Ms B's case, touching without consent can be unlawful. In that case there could have been two legal wrongs: a criminal wrong, such as assault, and a non-criminal (civil) wrong, such as trespass to the person, which was actually the claim Ms B succeeding in making. Ms B did not consent to the treatment; indeed, she vociferously refused to do so. The right to refuse something might be seen as the flip-side of the right to consent; without this, the right to consent looks devoid of meaning. Of course, when someone is refusing something as significant as life-supporting treatment, it is not unusual for questions to be asked about their right to do so.

Some such questions might be framed in terms of three important elements of consent (and refusal): capacity, information and freedom. First, we might presume (as some legal systems do) that adults generally have the mental capacity (or 'competence') required to take decisions about their own lives. But some people, such as those with advanced dementia, will lack this capacity. Others might lack the specific capacity for making the decision at hand: to draw an analogy, I might be judged competent to drive a car, but this does not mean that I am competent to pilot the *Millennium Falcon* spacecraft in *Star Wars*.

People might also lack important information, which is needed for the particular decision. 'Informed consent' is a prominent idea in modern medicine. Inaccurate or inadequate information might threaten the validity of any consent – and of any refusal to consent.

Finally, the decision – whether to accept or to reject treatment – must be sufficiently free, in the sense that it is voluntarily reached. Force, coercion or fraudulent misrepresentation of what is to occur might all cast doubt on the freedom, and thus the validity, of the decision reached.

But what if we have no such qualms, as indeed the judge concluded in relation to Ms B? Here was a competent and informed patient, deciding of her own volition that the unwanted treatment should cease. Should we necessarily grant such a wish? In order to explore this question, we need to look beneath consent and refusal, to the underlying principle: the principle of respect for autonomy.

▶ First among equals?

Autonomy, as we saw in Chapter 1, means self-rule. The associated principle is so esteemed that Raanan Gillon, a doctor and philosopher, labels it 'first among equals' (Gillon 2003). Its (subordinate?) 'equals', in Gillon's eyes, are the other three principles of biomedical ethics that were proposed by the American bioethicists Thomas Beauchamp and James Childress:

1 *beneficence*, which emphasizes obligations to provide patients with benefits and to balance benefits against risks;

2 *non-maleficence*, which concerns the obligation to avoid causing harm; and

3 *justice*, which insists on the fair distribution of benefits and risks between people (Beauchamp and Childress 2009).

Beneficence and non-maleficence might give us a useful steer when we have a patient, unlike Ms B, who lacks capacity. There will also be important questions of justice to consider, particularly given the expense associated with using ventilators and the like. But what of our central concern, respect for autonomy? The judge in Ms B's case observed that 'the principles of autonomy and beneficence would appear to be in conflict in this case'. She allowed autonomy to be her guide. But what should 'respect' for autonomy mean, in this case or any other?

▶ Give us our heart's desires?

John Coggon, who writes about English medical law, has usefully summarized three different versions of respecting autonomy (Coggon 2007):

1 *Current desire autonomy*. On this account, we respect autonomy by honouring a person's inclinations – even if, in the words of English law, the reasons behind these inclinations are irrational, unknown or entirely absent.

2 *Best desire autonomy*. Here we look more critically at what the person chooses. Is the choice consistent with who they are, their values and so forth? As some philosophers put it (Frankfurt 1971; Dworkin 1988), does the choice reflect their 'second-order' desires, such that they truly *want* to want this?

3 *Ideal desire autonomy.* Here we accept as genuinely autonomous only those choices that people *should* make, as judged against some objective set of values. On this view, we might disregard those choices that are incompatible with other values, such as (perhaps) preserving life.

We could reach different conclusions about Ms B's decision depending on which of these accounts we adopt. The first account seems to ask little of us: according to current desire autonomy, 'I want' seems to mean 'I should get', and all you need do (if anything) is check that I do indeed 'want' whatever is under consideration. There seem to be elements of this thinking in Dame Butler-Sloss's approach to the Ms B dilemma.

You seem more entitled to ask *why* I might want whatever I say I want when we move to best desire autonomy. Is my choice consistent with the person I am – with my 'world view' (Benjamin 1990)? If it is not, then you may have reason to override my decision. For her part, Ms B appeared from the evidence to be a fiercely independent individual, so her final choice seems entirely in keeping with the way she lived her life.

Ideal desire autonomy, however, invites us to reflect further on the content of our choices. Are we choosing the 'right' things? This has something of the Kantian concern with 'rational' behaviour (which we encountered in Chapter 1); indeed, Kant himself argued that the rational agent would not choose suicide. We might disagree about whether this is the correct label for what Ms B chose. Still, however we describe her choice, we are asked here to reflect on the validity of that choice.

▶ Take it to the limit?

While current desire autonomy seems to set the bar too low, such that virtually any choice merits respect, ideal desire autonomy might be thought to set it too high. Perhaps best desire autonomy is indeed best. But here, too, we need to consider whether there should be limits put on choices – even when these choices seem well considered.

One such limit again comes from Kant, who insisted that 'ought' implies 'can'. In other words, we cannot sensibly insist that something ought to happen, if this is impossible. Consider cardiopulmonary resuscitation (CPR). All too often, medical dramas depict the patient in cardiac arrest, who is saved by chest compressions and mouth-to-mouth resuscitation (Harris and Willoughby 2009). This certainly can happen. But for many patients CPR simply will not succeed in this way, because, for example, they are too frail or their heart stops in the course of a natural dying process. In short, CPR will not always work, which may explain why we less often see DNR ('do not resuscitate') orders nowadays, and more often encounter references to DNAR or DNACPR ('do not *attempt* resuscitation/CPR') – the most we can do is make the attempt, if it is right to do so.

So what if the patient insists on CPR, even if the doctors think she is one of those patients for whom the attempt is very likely to fail? If 'ought' implies 'can', then there seems to be no good reason for making the attempt, even in the name of respecting autonomy, since it looks as if it cannot work.

But there is another reason why we might resist such a demand. As we saw earlier, consent and refusal to consent appear to be closely related, since they concern the permission we grant others to interfere with us in some way (such as by performing surgery on us). A demand, however, goes further.

To see the differences, we need first to refer to Isaiah Berlin, who distinguished between 'negative' and 'positive' liberty (Berlin 1968). For Berlin, 'negative' liberty involved freedom from external restraint, while 'positive' liberty referred to the individual's capacity for 'self-mastery'. But some would say that there should still be limits on what even the 'self-mastering' individual should be free to choose or do. Using similar words to those used by Berlin, these thinkers distinguish between positive and negative *rights*. Negative rights require others to refrain from interfering with us; positive rights, meanwhile, seem to require some action by others. Once I have such rights, then the 'others' have corresponding *duties* (Hohfeld 1964). Here the differences seem to emerge: it is one thing to say 'don't do that', but surely quite another to instruct 'do that'.

Part of the problem with insisting 'do that' is that we might in turn interfere with what that person should themselves be free to do – with *their* negative rights.

And, according to John Stuart Mill, 'the only purpose for which power can be rightfully exercised over any member of a civilized community, against his will, is to prevent harm to others' (Warnock 1962: 135). So it seems that the autonomous individual is not entirely free – he or she must at least take due account of the autonomy and interests of others. Dame Elizabeth Butler-Sloss sought to do this when she recognized the rights of Ms B's care team not to be directly involved in a process to which they conscientiously objected. Indeed, Ms B also appeared alert to the interests of her loved ones. Unlike Anna, Ms B had declined to switch off the ventilator herself, as she did not want her godchild or her church 'to be worrying about whether it was suicide or not' (Laurance 2002).

Ms B's concerns seem to echo points made in relation to Gracie and Rosie Attard about the inadequacy of seeing autonomy as a matter of the 'atomized' individual. Some feminist scholars argue that models of 'relational autonomy' better acknowledge our connections (Mackenzie and Stoljar 2000). Relatedness, they claim, plays a huge role in who we are, and autonomy must therefore take due account of our social relations.

Ms B acknowledged the social web in which she resided. But she insisted that her own wishes took priority, over and above the feelings of her loved ones: 'There has been a lot of talking and crying as no one wants me to die but almost all of them empathize with me and my situation and sincerely wish to respect my wishes, which I have

made clear to all' (*Re B* (2003): para 52). Her friends –
and ultimately the doctors – felt bound to let Ms B be.

To what extent should such a patient's wishes bind?
We have seen some possible limits to the obligation,
particularly those that are reached when other people
come into the picture. But what if we restrict our focus
to the patient herself? Ms B's will was settled, and
her capacity to decide confirmed. What if her capacity
had been lacking, perhaps even permanently? How far
could her present autonomous self bind her future non-
autonomous self? This question forms the focus of the
next chapter.

4

Binding Odysseus

'...autonomy can grant us, here and now, the right to say "yes" – or instead "no" – to treatment. Some jurisdictions have extended this right to expressions of "precedent autonomy"; in other words, to the expressions we made before losing our autonomy.'

ALL THAT
MATTERS

Take me and bind me to the crosspiece half way up the mast; bind me as I stand upright, with a bond so fast that I cannot possibly break away, and lash the rope's ends to the mast itself. If I beg and pray you to set me free, then bind me more tightly still.
(Homer, *Odyssey*, Book XII (2009: 83))

As Odysseus approaches the rocks where Scylla and Charybdis reside, he hears the Sirens' song. Circe had warned him that to hear the song would render him incapable of rational thought. He instructs his crew to place wax in their ears and to bind him to the mast – an instruction he then seeks to revoke, on pain of death, when he hears the Sirens. In accordance with his prior wishes, the crew bind Odysseus still more firmly, until they are past danger.

▲ Did Odysseus make an advance directive so that he could resist the song of the Sirens?

Odysseus, it seems, had issued a 'living will' or 'advance directive' (Morgan 1994), which is sometimes also known, using Odysseus' Roman name, as a 'Ulysses contract'. Such directives are not unknown to today's patients and professionals. But whether or not they should be considered binding can be a complex question, as the following case from Canada reveals.

In that case: Georgette Malette

On 30 June 1979 Mrs Georgette Malette, then aged 57, was rushed into an emergency department in Ontario, following a road accident in which her husband had been killed. Mrs Malette was only semi-conscious and in a serious condition.

The doctors discovered that Mrs Malette was carrying a card that instructed 'NO BLOOD TRANSFUSION!' The card explained that she was a Jehovah's Witness, who was committed to the Bible's command: 'Keep abstaining ... from blood' (Acts 15: 28, 29). Mrs Malette's daughter, Celine, who arrived with her husband and a church elder, confirmed her mother's stated wish.

As Mrs Malette's condition worsened, the responsible doctor, Dr Shulman, felt he had to act, or else his patient would die. Aware of the card and the patient's wishes, Dr Shulman nevertheless proceeded to administer blood products. He reasoned that he could not be sure that the card conveyed Mrs Malette's current wishes, that she had been fully informed and not under pressure to sign the card, and that her refusal was to apply even when her life was at risk.

Mrs Malette made a good recovery, at which point she sued Dr Shulman and the hospital. She argued that, in overriding her wishes, the defendants had been negligent, had inflicted assault and battery on her, and had subjected her to religious discrimination. The judge agreed that Mrs Malette had been 'battered', for which she was due compensation. He stated:

> I ... find that the card is a written declaration of a valid position which the card carrier may legitimately take in imposing a written restriction on her contract with the doctor... The right to refuse treatment is an inherent component of the supremacy of the patient's right over his own body... However sacred life may be, fair social comment admits that certain aspects of life are properly held to be more important than life itself. (Malette v Shulman (1987))

The Ontario Court of Appeal upheld this decision, adding that 'the principal interest asserted by Mrs Malette in this case – the interest in the freedom to reject, or refuse to consent to, intrusions of her bodily integrity – outweighs the interest of the state in the preservation of life and health and the protection of the integrity of the medical profession' (Malette v. Shulman et al. (1990)).

▶ Preserving precedent autonomy

We saw in the previous chapter how autonomy can grant us, here and now, the right to say 'yes' – or 'no' – to treatment. Some jurisdictions have extended this right to expressions of 'precedent autonomy'; in other words, to the expressions we made before losing our autonomy, such as might occur when we lose the capacity currently to indicate our wishes.

The idea of a 'living will' was first proposed by an American attorney, Luis Kutner (1969). Nowadays, 'advance directive' tends to be the preferred term for a statement of wishes, usually made in writing, which specifies the types of treatment to which the drafter would object and the circumstances in which the directive is to apply.

Many American states have legislation providing for such directives, as do many countries worldwide, including Austria, Belgium, Germany, Singapore, England and Wales. In such jurisdictions, advance directives will often be considered binding – at least, provided that certain conditions are met. Other countries, such as France, Italy and Spain, see such directives as only advisory, rather than obligatory. Still other countries, including Greece, Ireland and Portugal, lack any particular laws in this area. Mindful of such variation and in keeping with its concern to protect human rights, the Council of Europe has recommended that advance directives be legally recognized across Europe.

Although there is some local variation, wherever advance directives are recognized as legally binding, there tend to be four criteria to meet, which will be familiar from Dr Shulman's concerns (and also from the previous chapter):

1 The directive should be made by someone with the requisite capacity;

2 That person should be appropriately well informed;

3 Their decision should be voluntary;

4 Perhaps crucially, the directive must clearly apply to the situation that has now arisen.

Many believe that such planning for the future is a good thing. Barack Obama himself has stated: 'I actually think it is a good idea to have a living will. I encourage everybody to get one. I have one. Michelle has one. We hope that we don't have to use it for a long time. But I think it is something that is sensible' (Obama 2009).

The idea certainly seems 'sensible' and should be uncontroversial. If, as I suggested in the previous chapter, consent and refusal are two sides of the same coin, then we have long recognized advance consent, so we should obviously endorse advance refusal, too. After all, patients undergoing surgical procedures under general anaesthetic obviously lack the capacity to say 'yes' *during* the procedure – the surgeon must rely on a previously issued permission. Surely the same should hold for a prior refusal?

▶ Is Odysseus bound?

Unfortunately, advance refusals can present problems, both in theory and in practice, such that they start to look less than 'sensible'. Let us start with the practical matters.

Two American scholars, Angela Fagerlin and Carl Schneider, think there are five reasons why policymakers should not invest too much effort in promoting advance directives:

1 Despite many efforts to educate and persuade, people rarely make such written statements – indeed, many people lack wills, let alone 'living wills'.

2 People do not know what they want. Decisions here and now are difficult enough; more difficult still are attempts 'to conjure up preferences for an unspecifiable future confronted with unidentifiable maladies with unpredictable treatments' (Fagerlin and Schneider 2004: 33).

3 People cannot specify what they want. This might explain why there have been recent pushes for setting down 'values histories' or 'advance care plans', which give more general guidance (which, in turn, might be criticized for lacking specificity).

4 Even if people can clear these hurdles, the directive might not be available when it is needed. Mrs Malette had a card on her person. Can everyone be relied on to carry such a statement?

5 The ultimate decision-maker – such as the doctor – still might not interpret the directive 'accurately' (assuming that there is an accurate reading available). Research from the UK shows that one and same directive can be open to quite different interpretations (Thompson, Barbour and Schwartz 2003). Even if one opts for a permanent tattoo (Polack 2001), stating 'not for resuscitation', is this enough for the doctor to go on?

For Fagerlin and Schneider, advance directives are not necessarily worth the paper – or skin – they may (or may not) be written on.

▶ Who's binding who?

Perhaps, then, many advance directives will fail to preserve autonomy in the way they intend. In any case, it is not altogether clear that autonomy should always trump other values, such as preserving life. The reticence of some doctors, like Dr Shulman, may be understandable, if we admit that there may be conflicting duties. Doctors in France, for example, appear reluctant to abandon vulnerable patients (Horn 2012).

Of course, such an argument could become too paternalistic, if autonomous wishes are ousted by a concern with the patient's welfare, no matter what the patient might say to the contrary. But we can still question how far autonomy should be extended. Should *demands* for future treatment, issued in advance of incapacity, be honoured? The English courts certainly thought not, because Leslie Burke, a patient with a degenerative neurological disorder, was denied the right to dictate that life-sustaining food and fluids, delivered by artificial means, should be provided to him once he had lost the ability to communicate (*R (on the application of Burke) v General Medical Council* (2005)). The court nevertheless still sought to retain some measure of Mr Burke's autonomy, insisting that his wishes should at least be consulted at the critical time.

And there is a fresh problem here. Why should the current (competent) Mr Burke bind the future (incompetent) Mr Burke? People's views change. Even those who appear firmly committed to a particular set of principles can alter their allegiances. Another ruling from England amply illustrates this, because in that case 'Ms AE' was raised Muslim but she later became a Jehovah's Witness (*HE v A Hospital NHS Trust* (2003)).

Like Mrs Malette, Ms AE issued an advance directive, declining blood products 'in *any* circumstances'. When she became critically ill, however, her father argued that the directive should be ignored, because his daughter was preparing to follow the Muslim faith once more. The judge found the evidence compelling; he agreed that the directive could not stand and that life-saving treatment could be given.

Even when there is no evidence of such significant shifts, there remains the argument that the incompetent person is not the same person who drafted the directive. The issues here are not quite those that concern personhood in the sense we explored in Chapter 2. Rather, here, philosophers perceive a problem in terms of 'personal identity'. They ask: 'Who am I?' and 'What makes me *me*?' Their answers tend to fall into one of three groups.

First, there are those who emphasize bodily continuity. For them, a significant aspect of our identity resides in our physical make-up – our distinctive faces, fingerprints and DNA, and maybe even our tattoos, piercings and haircuts. This explains why, in the film *Face/Off* (1997), John Travolta's criminal mastermind is able to pass himself off as Nicholas Cage's police officer, after undergoing a face transplant procedure. (This procedure has since departed the realm of science fiction and entered science fact – however, unlike in the film, the recipients of such transplants do not entirely resemble their donors (Huxtable and Woodley 2005).)

Others reject the emphasis on the body because they believe that personal identity is located in more metaphysical properties. The French philosopher René Descartes (1596–1650) famously distinguished between the 'body' and the 'mind' (or 'soul'). Philosophers who have subsequently adopted this 'Cartesian dualism' tend to think that the mind is in charge – and that it is this which provides the key to identity.

So, they say, psychological continuity is what counts: the enduring presence of a functioning brain, personality, 'world view' and memory make me *me*. For them, this better explains *Face/Off* (1997): despite adopting the other's face, the film's protagonists fundamentally remain who they are. It also better explains what is going on when we have our hair cut, gain piercings and even choose our outfits – we are trying to express who we are.

But psychological continuity seems to present a problem for advance directives. Why does the competent person who prepared the directive have authority over the body of the future incompetent individual? If we think that these are different individuals (and that this is morally problematic), then perhaps we should redirect our attention to the body. But this also does not seem to work, because we cannot be absolutely certain that the body persists over time. Scientists tell us, for example, that our cells regenerate every seven years. So is there a whole new me every seven years?

Maybe we should not get too hung up on these questions. Indeed, the neurologist Antonio Damasio has argued that it is wrong to try to separate mind from body, and rationality from the emotions (Damasio 1995). He points to a third way of thinking about identity, in which mind and body are inseparable; we are 'embodied' selves. As Alastair Campbell (forthcoming) notes, Roy Porter has put this position beautifully, when writing about the themes he detected in Lawrence Sterne's eighteenth-century novel *The Life and Opinions of Tristram Shandy, Gentleman* (Sterne 2003):

> *With its own elaborate sign-language of gesture and feeling, the body was the inseparable dancing-partner of the mind or soul – now in step, now a tangle of limbs and intentions, mixed emotions. Organism and consciousness, soma and psyche, heart and head, the outer and the inner – all merged, and all needed to be minutely observed, if the human enigma were ever to be appreciated.* (Porter 2003: 294)

This account of the 'human enigma' looks appealing. But it still does not solve our dilemma about whether the competent me is – and can therefore bind – the incompetent me; it tells us only that mind and body (together) matter.

It seems we cannot solve this here. But what we probably can say is that the prior me seems to have *some* claim on what happens to the future me. Every day we take decisions that affect our future lives (however minor), on the assumption that we will continue to exist (for at least some time) beyond the now. Respecting such decisions appears to be consistent with the commitment to honouring autonomy, particularly if you recall my general anaesthetic example. After all, if the competent me cannot advance a claim over the incompetent me, who can? Doctors? Family members? We will revisit these groups in the next chapter.

We have surveyed a number of problems with advance directives, both theoretical and practical. Some of these appeared to be considerable. But perhaps they should not be overstated: there will be situations, such as when we near the end of a gruesomely predictable disease trajectory, in which we can specify clearly, in advance, what we do not want. The evidence suggests that we would do well to make our instructions as explicit as possible. But what if we fail to do so or we make no advance statement of any kind? We will pick up this question next.

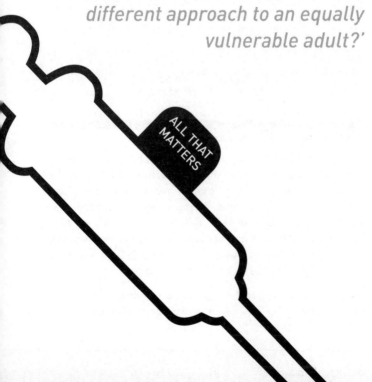

5

Twilight worlds

'If we failed to feed a baby, we could expect to answer for our neglect in court. So why should we take a different approach to an equally vulnerable adult?'

ALL THAT
MATTERS

'You see George, you've really had a wonderful life. Don't you see what a mistake it would be to just throw it away?'

In that perennial festive favourite, the film *It's a Wonderful Life* (1946), Clarence the angel earns his wings by showing George – who was contemplating suicide – how wonderful his life is. The story ends with George convinced that his life should continue, and the friends and family he had previously helped now coming to George's aid.

Of course, life is not always wonderful and – try as they might – loved ones cannot always help to make it so. What counts as a wonderful (or even a satisfactory) life has lain at the heart of numerous recent court decisions worldwide. Some of the hardest cases concern individuals who have lost all or most of their ability to communicate with the outside world. Terri Schiavo's story is a particularly well-known example.

In that case: Terri Schiavo

On 25 February 1990, 26-year-old Terri Schiavo collapsed in her Florida home. In hospital, it was discovered that Terri's brain had been deprived of oxygen. After Terri was judged incompetent, her husband Michael was appointed her guardian. Within a year Terri was diagnosed as being in a persistent vegetative state, which meant that, although she had periods of sleeping and waking, she remained unconscious. A feeding tube kept her alive.

When Michael requested an order against attempting resuscitation, Terri's parents, Mr and Mrs Schindler, objected. They also disagreed with his view that tube feeding should cease. Mr Schiavo relinquished his guardianship role and the matter came to court in early 2000. In court, Terri's parents insisted that, as a Roman Catholic, their daughter would want treatment to continue. Her husband, however, said Terri had indicated that she would not value life in a condition like this. The court favoured Michael's conclusion.

Although the tube was withdrawn on 24 April 2001, it was reinstated two days later, when the issues returned to court. New evidence was heard about Terri's condition. The judge, however, was unconvinced by evidence, put forward by the Schindlers, that Terri was not in a vegetative state. On appeal, the senior judge also upheld the decision to withdraw the feeding tube. Once more the tube was withdrawn, on 15 October 2003. But, once again, it was reinstated, this time when Florida's governor, Jeb Bush, passed a law allowing him to intervene. One year later the Florida Supreme Court found that law to be unconstitutional.

By 2005 Terri's story was known worldwide. The Schindlers continued to petition the courts for different therapies and tests, which the judge did not consider to be appropriate for Terri. On 18 March 2005 the feeding tube was again withdrawn. By this time even the President, George W. Bush, had become involved, with jurisdiction over the case being passed from the state to the federal courts.

The saga therefore ended in the Supreme Court, which found that the Schindlers had no more avenues open to them. Terri died on 31 March 2005, surrounded by police officers, who were there to ensure that no attempt was made to restart feeding (Huxtable 2012: 51–4).

▶ Twilight worlds?

A patient like Terri Schiavo might be said to occupy a 'twilight world' (as one British judge put it), existing somewhere between life and death (*NHS Trust v I* (2003)). In many countries death is defined as the loss of brainstem function (Academy of Medical Royal Colleges 2008). Patients in the vegetative state have lost higher brain function – and so might never again interact meaningfully with the world – but their brainstems will be intact. They can therefore be expected to live for many years – provided, that is, that they are given appropriate support, like tube feeding.

The vegetative state is not the only 'twilight' state. It is one of several 'disorders of consciousness' (as defined by the Multi-Society Task Force on PVS 1994, and the Royal College of Physicians 2003). These disorders include:

▶ *coma*, which is a state of unconsciousness, without any wakefulness (and therefore no sleep–wake cycles). A prolonged coma is very rare: the condition usually lasts for hours or days, until the patient recovers or moves into a different state, such as...

▶ the *vegetative state*, from which the patient can also recover, although (like Terri Schiavo) he or she might stay in this condition until death. The state may be labelled 'persistent' after four weeks. The state may then be labelled 'permanent' after either three or six months (according to different guidelines) following non-traumatic brain injury, or one year after traumatic brain injury.

▶ the *minimally conscious state* (sometimes called the 'low awareness' state and originally labelled the 'minimally responsive' state) involves minimal but detectable evidence of awareness. Patients might move from the vegetative state into this state; some recover, but others remain here.

All of these states rob the patients of their capacity to decide on what should or should not happen with their bodies. Yet recent research has revealed that some patients who were diagnosed as being in the vegetative state actually showed signs of consciousness (Owen et al. 2006; Monti et al. 2010), while others appeared more responsive when they were given a sleeping pill (Clauss and Nel 2006). Diagnosis is complex and the lines between states can be difficult to discern. Even if they agree on the diagnosis, scientists can disagree about what this means: for example, some maintain that there are 'degrees' of minimal consciousness, while others insist there is only one category here (Bruno et al. 2011; *W v. M and S and A NHS Primary Care Trust* (2011)).

Little wonder, then, that the courts have been called on to settle questions pertaining to such patients, especially those in the vegetative state. The cases began in the US, with Karen Ann Quinlan in the 1970s (*In re Quinlan* (1976)), and have spread worldwide, to such patients as Anthony Bland in England (*Airedale NHS Trust v Bland* (1993)), Eluana Englaro in Italy (Luchetti 2010) and Erika Küllmer in Germany (Jox 2011). The uncertainty and complexity mean the judges' task is not easy, particularly when they confront so fundamental a question as whether to treat or not to treat.

▶ To treat or not to treat?

Some critics, like John Keown (2002), warn us not to be beguiled into talking of treatment and non-treatment. Really, they say, the question in a case like Terri's is: to feed or not to feed? And they fail to see why a distinction should be drawn between cups and spoons, on the one hand, and tubes, on the other. If we failed to feed a baby, we could expect to answer for our neglect in court. So why should we take a different approach to an equally vulnerable adult? We see something of this argument in the Schindlers' opposition to feeding being removed from their daughter.

This is not to say that Roman Catholics, or other adherents to the intrinsic value of life, will insist that feeding or treatment should always continue. In this tradition, disproportionate or futile attempts to prolong life may be avoided. But this is only one perspective on what we might consider to be in the 'best interests' of incapacitated patients. David DeGrazia has helpfully described three ways of thinking about this decision-making standard, which we might summarize as follows:

1 *Mental-state welfare.* Here, our welfare, and thus our best interests, consists in having particular positive mental states, like happiness or the avoidance of suffering;

2 *Preference welfare.* Here, our welfare is served when our preferences are satisfied. This obviously connects up with ideas about autonomy;

3 *Objective welfare.* On this account, there are some objective 'goods', such as life itself, so our welfare consists in having these goods (DeGrazia 1995).

None of these approaches is trouble-free. Mental-state welfare seems incapable of condemning the undesired but painless death. It also fails to tell us what (if anything) is wrong with a situation where our positive mental state is not to be trusted. Consider, for example, the film *The Matrix* (1999), in which the protagonists' reality is a sham, constructed by machines to which their bodies are connected.

Preference welfare, meanwhile, runs into some of autonomy's problems. Which preferences count as 'good'? What if we don't know that our preferences have been satisfied – have we still benefited in some way? And what if we do not have or have not expressed our preferences about the matter at hand?

Objective welfare runs into similar difficulty, because who is to say which 'objective goods' count? Why should life be considered a good in this way, especially if the person living that life wants it to end?

You might detect, beneath each of these accounts, our familiar perspectives on the value of life. Preference welfare seems inclined towards the self-determined value of life, objective welfare towards the intrinsic value of life (at least when life is one of the objective goods listed). Mental-state welfare, meanwhile, resembles the instrumental value of life, in its preoccupation with happiness and the like – or with what some call the 'quality of life'.

Quality of life is another complex notion, as indeed we saw in Chapter 2. Adherents to the instrumental value of life take this idea furthest, when they claim that very poor-quality lives can be ended. Indeed, Peter Singer thinks that patients like Terri Schiavo cease to be persons in a morally relevant sense. Better, then, to end such impoverished lives, even by lethal injection. Although most legal systems are nowhere near that point, Singer thinks we are living through a 'revolution' over the value of life, in which legal judgements like that in Terri's case signal the dismantling of our commitment to the sanctity of life (Singer 1994).

But those who remain so committed resist Singer's arguments. Otherwise, where is the line to be drawn? Incapacity can take many forms: disorders of consciousness are among the most severe examples, but one's capacity to make decisions can also be diminished or even removed by such conditions as dementia. Even those who generally have capacity might lack the specific capacity to take particular decisions or perform particular tasks (like me lacking the skills to pilot the *Millennium Falcon*).If the instrumental value of life is our guide, then which of these differently incapacitated patients is to live and which is to die?

In contrast, scholars like Keown argue that all incapacitated individuals still count as persons who are worthy of protection and respect. In a similar vein, the Nuffield Council on Bioethics in the UK has argued that *solidarity* means that we should help vulnerable others, in recognition of the fact that we, too, might have been –or one day will be – in similar need (Prainsack and Buyx 2011). *It's a Wonderful Life* offers a vivid depiction of solidarity in action.

Some scientists believe that the very labels used in this area need to be revised, and their belief seems rooted in such notions of respect. So, they say, we should do away with references to the 'vegetative state', with its implication that here lies a 'vegetable', and replace them with terms like 'post-coma unresponsiveness' (National Health and Medical Research Council 2004) or 'unresponsive wakefulness syndrome' (Laureys et al. 2010).

The judges, for their part, seem to move between the intrinsic and the instrumental value of life. Reference will be made, in a case like Terri Schiavo's, to what the patient might be assumed to want. Yet, whether it is the patient's assumed view or that of some other decision-maker, instrumental considerations often come to the fore. A life like Terri Schiavo's tends to be seen as particularly lacking, so emphasis is placed on the instrumental value of life, and the decision is made to stop treatment (or, if you prefer, feeding). It remains to be seen whether emerging scientific findings about the alleged retention of consciousness in such patients will convince the judges to take a different approach. Certainly, elsewhere, such as when the patient is in a minimally conscious state, the glimmerings of awareness can incline the judges towards upholding the intrinsic value of life, and thus towards continued treatment.

Whether the judges are taking the right approaches is an open question. Also open to question is their right to decide such cases. So who should have the final right of say?

▶ Who decides?

Judges might seem well placed to decide on issues of life and death, particularly if the people directly involved cannot reach agreement. There will be other sources of advice available to them, such as clinical ethicists or clinical ethics committees, which exist in many hospitals. Indeed, such individuals and committees are there mainly to offer advice – rather than an instruction – in ethically difficult cases.

But it might be thought that there are already people entitled to steer the final decision: the loved ones of the incapacitated patient. Many legal systems provide for the appointment of 'proxies' or 'surrogate decision-makers'. In England and Wales, for example, under the Mental Capacity Act 2005, I can confer a 'lasting power of attorney' on my wife, Genevieve, which would enable her to make decisions on my behalf, in the event of me losing capacity. The courts can similarly appoint people on my behalf, as was the case in Terri's situation, in which Michael was named guardian.

Surrogates look like a sensible, and ethically defensible, phenomenon. Who could know me better than my wife? She might therefore be well placed to make what is called a 'substituted judgement' on my behalf – a decision that

I could be expected to take, in view of my values, if I had the capacity to do so. Such a decision might approach the 'preference' version of my best interests. It might therefore link with notions like relational autonomy, to which we referred in Chapter 3, and also with the idea of 'narrative ethics', in which close attention to the story of my life can point to ways out of ethically complex situations (McCarthy 2003).

But, of course, there are many others who can claim to know me and my story. My sisters, Jackie and Kerry, might form their own views about where my interests lie, and they might point to conversations never had with Genevieve in which I reached a different conclusion to the one she now reaches. And then my friends Lynette and Alex might intervene, saying that all of these parties are biased, given the inheritance they might expect to gain from my passing, if that is what the final decision is to mean. Should we dismiss all voices but Genevieve's, if she is whom I chose to make these critical decisions? (And, I might add, how are we adequately to account for *her* interests and how these might be affected by the decision?)

So even surrogate decision-making is complex. We cannot necessarily avoid these difficulties by vesting authority in the doctors and their teams. They will, often quite rightly, have a view informed by their specific expertise – and not necessarily by my wider interests, whether cultural, familial or spiritual. It seems, then, that we need a place in which these different voices can be heard – which might well be an ethics committee or a court. We will return to these issues in Chapter 10.

Whosoever ultimately decides, their decision will need to be rooted in some understanding of what is best for me. As we have seen, there is a plurality of perspectives on what counts as serving (or compromising) an incapacitated patient's best interests. We have focused here on adults. We might think that things will be easier when the patient is a child, because there is a more obvious authority figure: the parent. We will test the accuracy of this hypothesis in the next chapter, in which we move to consider critically ill infants.

6

Critical decisions

'There are numerous conditions, affecting every part of the body, which might cause a child to need some sort of specialist care. But when (if ever) might we say that the disability is too onerous for that child to bear?'

ALL THAT
MATTERS

> *Life and death are... balanced on the edge of a razor.*
> (Homer, *Iliad*, Book X (2006: 79))

Homer's observation in the *Iliad* appears all too applicable to some infants, such as those born prematurely, for whom critical care decisions must be taken. Such decisions can raise agonizing questions for the child's parents and the health care team. One book phrases the central issue in particularly stark terms: *Should the Baby Live?* (Kuhse and Singer 1985). This question lay at the heart of court proceedings in England concerning the fate of Charlotte Wyatt.

In that case: Charlotte Wyatt

Born three months prematurely on 21 October 2003, Charlotte Wyatt was found to have brain damage and serious problems with her heart, lungs and kidneys. Charlotte had to be resuscitated three times in the first ten months of her life. By this point she was reliant on an oxygen box in order to breathe.

The doctors judged the situation to be intolerable for Charlotte, who would be unlikely to see, hear or develop further. They approached the High Court for permission not to intervene, should Charlotte suffer a fourth crisis. As they made known in the national press, Charlotte's parents thought that their daughter should be given the chance of life. So began a long-running legal saga, in which the case came to court on at least 11 occasions.

In the first hearing, Mr Justice Hedley decided that it would not be in Charlotte's best interests to attempt resuscitation and provide artificial ventilation. His view did not change a few months later: although Charlotte seemed stronger, the judge doubted that she could survive such invasive treatment.

Against expectations, Charlotte did survive the winter of 2004 and by the spring she had improved further, needing less oxygen support. But her neurological condition remained bleak, her lungs still struggled, and she was malnourished, because she could not easily tolerate food. The judge again confirmed that artificial ventilation would be 'futile' and should be avoided.

Hedley's decisions were upheld in a superior court, the Court of Appeal, in the autumn of 2005. The judges confirmed that the 'best interests' of the child were the court's paramount consideration, as judged from the assumed perspective of the individual child, and taking an appropriately wide interpretation of those interests. A judge might therefore draw up a 'balance sheet' of considerations for and against treatment, before deciding where the balance should fall. The judges in the appeal court thought that Mr Justice Hedley had taken the right approach to Charlotte's care and they hoped that, under Hedley's guidance, the parties might now be able to agree on a treatment plan for Charlotte.

So the issues were returned to Mr Justice Hedley. He declined to give the doctors the final say but he also refused to force them to abide by whatever the Wyatts might wish to occur. He therefore recognized the professionals' rights conscientiously to object to involvement in anything they considered contrary to Charlotte's interests. Ideally, he hoped, the parties could work together, as and when any crisis arose.

When a crisis occurred in 2006, however, the parties returned to the courtroom. After some improvements, and even some visits home, Charlotte had deteriorated again. Hedley refused to issue an instruction: he left it to the doctors to decide, at the critical time, whether ventilation would be right for Charlotte (Huxtable 2012: 33-6).

▲ Charlotte Wyatt

The last we know about Charlotte is that, as 2010 neared, she had been out of hospital for two years. By this point she was living in foster care, where she was learning to walk. Charlotte may have developed but she was evidently left with considerable disabilities. This is not uncommon in children born at the 'borderline of viability'. The phrase was used by the UK's Nuffield Council on Bioethics (2006) to describe extremely premature babies – those who are born under 26 weeks of gestation, when pregnancy usually lasts 40 weeks. In 2004–5, 1,600 of 584,000 deliveries in England were on this borderline. Although some of these babies will die, others do survive. The 1995 UK-wide EPICure study found the following rates of survival to discharge from hospital:

▶ born between 22 to 23 weeks: 1%

▶ born between 23 to 24 weeks: 11%

▶ born between 24 to 25 weeks: 26%

▶ born between 25 to 26 weeks: 44%

Survival rates appear to have improved since. However, these data still give useful advice to parents about the likelihood of their child having disabilities if they survive. Children in the last group tend to have no or only mild disabilities. Children born earlier, however, are very likely to have moderate or severe disabilities.

Of course, it is not only premature babies who might live with a disability. There are numerous conditions, affecting every part of the body, that might cause a child to need some sort of specialist care. But when (if ever) might we say that the disability is too onerous for that child to bear? When should the child live – and when might the child be allowed to die?

▶ Guiding principles?

Mindful of the dilemmas that can arise, the Royal College of Paediatrics and Child Health (2004) has provided a framework for deciding about when to withhold or withdraw life-sustaining treatment from critically ill children. The Royal College describes five situations when treatment might be limited:

1 When the child is *brain-dead* (and thus no longer legally alive);

2 When the child is in a *permanent vegetative state*, and the court authorizes the removal of treatment;

3 The *'no chance' situation*, where 'the child has such severe disease that life-sustaining treatment simply delays death without significant alleviation of suffering';

4 The *'no purpose' situation*, where 'although the patient may be able to survive with treatment, the degree of physical or mental impairment will be so great that it is unreasonable to expect them to bear it';

5 The *'unbearable' situation*, in which 'the child and/ or family feel that, in the face of progressive and irreversible illness, further treatment is more than can be borne [although] it may be of some benefit'.

The guidance recommends safeguarding the child's life wherever there is significant uncertainty or disagreement, at least until such issues are resolved. It adds that withdrawing treatment does not signal abandonment: some care will still be given, including palliative care, that is aimed at making the child comfortable in what time he or she has left.

▶ Futile treatments?

The 'no chance', 'no purpose' and 'unbearable' situations recall a principle we encountered earlier, which is associated with the intrinsic value of life. According to this principle, a distinction may be drawn between a 'proportionate' and a 'disproportionate' response to a patient's suffering. Intervention is disproportionate if either the anticipated benefits are outweighed by the anticipated burdens or (in the words of Mr Justice Hedley) it will be 'futile'. Here, intervention is not required. Proportionate responses, meanwhile, can be expected to do more good than ill – and these will be morally obligatory, because they reflect the sanctity of human life.

This principle helps to distinguish the intrinsic value of life from 'vitalism', in which life is granted an absolute value, requiring every effort for its preservation. The intrinsic value of life instead recognizes that there are limits. The poet Arthur Hugh Clough satirized the limits defined by the disproportionate/proportionate distinction: 'Thou shalt not kill; but need'st not strive | Officiously to keep alive' (quoted in Singer 1994: 194). The concept of 'futility' tries to define the 'officious' limits, but it is open to criticism.

Robert Halliday (1997) says that futility can be understood in *quantitative* and *qualitative* terms. Qualitatively, a 'futile' treatment may be said to produce an effect but this effect is not 'beneficial' for the patient because, for example, he or she will continue to endure a poor quality of life, Quantitatively, meanwhile, we may deem a treatment 'futile' if experience indicates that the probability of producing the beneficial effect is low. But how low does this probability need to be? What if I am in the 1 per cent of patients who might be expected to benefit – surely, if it means I might live, I would judge that to be a chance worth taking? And what is the evidence on which we might base this conclusion?

Philosophers also complain that the judgement of 'futility' fallaciously moves from an 'is' (treatment *is* unlikely to have a beneficial effect) to an 'ought' (such treatment *ought not* to be given). But what ought to occur is precisely what we're trying to work out. Patients and their families, meanwhile, might complain that the judgement is inappropriate, because it views the idea of 'benefit' in starkly medical terms, in which the body is a machine.

What about serving other values, like offering hope to the patient and their loved ones? These visitors to the critical care wards are unlikely to welcome talk of 'futility', with its connotations of 'uselessness' (Gillon 1997).

Behind the label, then, are big questions about the benefits and goals of health care. Proponents of the futility model want to insist that their central concern is with respecting life and that withholding or withdrawing 'futile' treatment merely recognizes the proper limits of that obligation. They are not, they say, committed to a vitalistic insistence on preserving life at all costs. But opponents detect a quite different ethic at work, which either these proponents must embrace or, if they truly wish to preserve life, they must be forced into taking the vitalist line. This alternative ethic, it should be no surprise to learn, views life in terms of its *instrumental* value.

▶ Futile lives?

Taken to its extreme, the instrumental value of life signals that a life of inability or disability might rightly be ended. The focus therefore shifts from futile treatments to futile lives. As we saw in the previous chapter, quality-of-life considerations are at the heart of this approach.

According to its defenders, these considerations really underlie guidance like that from the Royal College. The defenders therefore want to go further, dismantling the distinction between 'acts' and 'omissions' and abolishing illusory references to 'futility' and the like.

James Rachels (1997) has famously sought to discredit the act/omission distinction, to which the intrinsic value of life clings, by means of a thought experiment. Imagine two cousins, he says, called Smith and Jones. Each intends to end the life of another, younger cousin, in order to receive an inheritance. The cousin is taking a bath. Smith enters the bathroom and holds the boy's head under the water until he drowns. Jones, meanwhile, walks in with the same aim but he sees the child slip, hit his head and fall unconscious into the water. The boy drowns, because Jones declines to rescue him.

Rachels sees these situations as ethically identical: the intention and outcome is the same, but Smith acts, while Jones refrains from acting. This leads Rachels to abandon the distinction and to argue that, as acts and omissions are indistinguishable, both should be allowed in order to end lives of particularly poor quality.

According to this logic, Dutch doctors in Groningen are right to have drafted a protocol that permits the lives of seriously ill children to be ended, including by positive action (Manninen 2006). The protocol permits such euthanasia where the child is enduring 'hopeless and unbearable suffering' and the parents consent.

For many, these arguments – and the Groningen protocol – go too far. Rachels' experiment has been criticized for being significantly removed from the realities of clinical practice (Forbes 1998). And alternative thought experiments, while also some distance from the clinic, can provide support for the act/omission distinction. Oxford philosopher and clinician Tony Hope refers to

Robinson and Davies (Hope 2000). Robinson does not donate to a famine-stricken country, which means that one life is not saved. Davies, however, does donate, thereby saving one life – but he also sends a poisoned food parcel, which kills one person. The same number of lives is lost, but Davies has also saved one life – so hasn't he acted best? Our intuition would probably tell us not, because sending the poisoned parcel looks worse than not sending a donation.

Defenders of the distinction think that Robinson need not be held to account for his omission in the same way as Davies might for his action. For one thing, Robinson need not have *intended* his omission to have a particular (bad) effect, such as a person dying. He might have *foreseen* this, but the doctrine of double effect, introduced in Chapter 1, tells us that merely foreseeing bad is less problematic than intending to achieve bad. Similarly, a doctor might only intend to remove burdensome treatments that are interfering with a patient's natural dying process.

If we hold people to account for every omission, then it may be difficult to draw the line where their responsibility for omissions stops. There is always a multitude of things we are not doing, sometimes quite knowingly. Indeed, we might not be the agents responsible for an outcome. This idea is captured in the phrase 'letting nature take its course', in which 'nature' might ultimately be deemed responsible for certain outcomes, rather than, say, the doctors who have failed to hold nature at bay.

There is much to commend in these counter-arguments. But still there lingers the suspicion that some omissions will be virtually indistinguishable from acts. Contrast 'pulling out the feeding tube' with 'no longer supplying feed down a tube' – the behaviours appear indistinguishable, but the first looks much more active than the second. Unsurprisingly, Tony Hope himself admits that he keeps changing his mind about the validity of the act/omission distinction.

▶ Who decides?

No matter how we might judge the act/omission distinction and thus a protocol like that adopted in Groningen, we can at least commend the protocol for leaving the final decision with the child's parents. This also happens on wards where the critical decision concerns only withholding care, rather than actively ending life.

Studies reveal that parents can play an influential role in decision-making (Cuttini et al. 1999), but they also indicate that doctors and nurses judge critical decisions to be too burdensome for parents (Boyle, Salter and Arnander 2004). Yet parents who have spent a great deal of time in intensive-care units seem very equipped to make even these decisions (McHaffie 2001). Sometimes the child him- or herself will be so equipped. For example, after enduring a great deal of treatment, at the age of 13 Hannah Jones was deemed competent by her parents and doctors to refuse a life-saving heart transplant (Weaver 2009).

Hannah later reversed her decision and says she is glad she did so. But what is important is that she was judged capable of making a crucial decision for herself. Autonomy, you will recall, can be considered decision-specific. We should not forget that children and young people will increasingly develop the capacity to make decisions – even though, unlike Hannah, they are seldom allowed (at least in law) to say when life-saving treatment should cease.

Generally, however, decisions about the care of young patients turn on their best interests. How these assessments should be made will involve some of the questions we encountered in the previous chapter – although, for the infant who has never formed any views whatsoever, an approach based on 'substituted judgement' will be much less helpful. Elsewhere, the assessments will engage with familiar themes of life, choice and avoiding suffering. Unsurprisingly, these themes appear again in the next chapter, in which we consider how palliative care can ease the dying process.

7

Peaceful endings

'Specialists in palliative care intend neither to postpone nor to hasten death – they intend to relieve suffering.'

ALL THAT
MATTERS

To sleep: perchance to dream: ay, there's the rub;
For in that sleep of death what dreams may come
When we have shuffled off this mortal coil.

Shakespeare's famous passage in *Hamlet* (Act III, scene i) invokes the sleep of death but, nowadays, when a patient's pain, suffering or distress is unremitting, the transition from life to death might actually be eased by sleep itself – or, at least, something resembling sleep. Palliative medicine is capable of tackling even the most difficult symptoms, using potent opioid drugs like morphine. When even these fail, sedative drugs may be given to ensure that the patient is no longer aware of pain or distress and to allow a peaceful end. But the line between ending pain and ending life can appear perilously thin, as the following case demonstrates.

In that case: Dr John Bodkin Adams

Dr John Bodkin Adams was a GP in England. Amid allegations that he had inherited under his patients' wills, Adams was investigated and then charged with the murder of Mrs Edith Morrell.

▲ Dr John Bodkin Adams

Mrs Morrell had suffered a stroke and also had cerebral arteriosclerosis, a condition which causes headaches, facial pain and impaired vision. An autopsy revealed high levels of barbiturates and of opioids like morphine. Dr Adams's lawyers insisted that he had intended to kill only the patient's pain – not the patient.

Dr Adams made legal history: not only did he decline to take the stand in his own defence, but his was the trial in which an important principle was first expressed in English law. Directing the jury, Mr Justice Devlin explained that the law of murder applies just as much to the dying as to the healthy, and that it binds everyone, including doctors. But, he added, 'If the first purpose of medicine, the restoration of health, can no longer be achieved there is still much for a doctor to do, and he is entitled to do all that is proper and necessary to relieve pain and suffering, even if the measures he takes may incidentally shorten life.'

The jury retired to consider their verdict. They returned just 43 minutes later to declare the doctor innocent. Plans to prosecute Adams over the deaths of other patients were dropped and the GP returned to practice (Huxtable 2007: 84–114).

Mr Justice Devlin's direction brought the doctrine of double effect explicitly into English law. The idea has since been adopted in many other legal systems. As we saw in Chapter 2, the principle distinguishes between intending and (merely) foreseeing a 'bad' outcome like death. Foreseen 'bad' effects may be allowed, when four conditions are met:

1 The act itself is good, or at least neutral;

2 The good effect is not obtained by means of the bad one;

3 The bad effect is not intended, but only foreseen and permitted; and

4 There is a proportionately strong reason for permitting the bad effect.

In theory, the principle has wide relevance in health care. Surgeons, for example, cut into bodies and cause scarring and tissue damage. However, their intention is good – it is, for example, to remove a tumour and we might think that the other ('bad') effects are merely incidental. Yet, rightly or wrongly, the principle tends to be most associated with palliative care, which has its roots in the hospice movement pioneered in England by Dame Cicely Saunders. The World Health Organization defines palliative care as:

> *an approach that improves the quality of life of patients and their families facing the problem associated with life-threatening illness, through the prevention and relief of suffering by means of early identification and impeccable assessment and treatment of pain and other problems, physical, psychosocial and spiritual.* (WHO 2013)

Specialists in palliative care intend neither to postpone nor to hasten death – they intend to relieve suffering. Devlin's principle is said to be useful here because the drugs used to relieve symptoms can have a double effect: they are also capable of suppressing breathing, and thus potentially shortening life.

▶ Innocent intentions?

Supporters of the intrinsic value of life claim that the double-effect principle captures a crucial moral difference between intending and foreseeing harm:

> *Imagine a potholer stuck with two people behind him and the water rising to drown them. And suppose two cases: in one he can be blown up; in the other a rock can be moved to open an escape route but it will crush him to death... There might be people... who, seeing the consequence, would move the rock, though they would not blow up the man because that would be choosing his death as the means of escape. This is a far from meaningless stance, for they thus show themselves as people who will absolutely reject any policy making the death of innocent people a means or end.* (Gormally 1994: 49)

Critics find this unconvincing and self-serving, because the principle seems to succeed only if we describe the situation as the supporters wish. Could we not equally say that crushing the potholer involves 'choosing his death as the means of escape'?

The critics therefore think that the supporters load the dice: they choose a description that enables them to reach the result they want, in which they pretend that the forbidden result is only 'incidental' or 'foreseen'. This implies that the result, rather than the rule, informs their thinking, which suggests that the supporters owe more to consequentialist (outcome-driven) reasoning than to deontological (duty-driven) reasoning. And, if that is the case, then the supporters should openly toe the consequentialist line and admit that death can be a good outcome in some cases – which will require them also to accept the case for assisted dying.

The critics therefore detect problems in double-effect reasoning that are similar to those that undermined references to 'disproportionate' and 'futile' treatment. When double effect is applied to drugs like morphine, the supporters seem to be saying that it can be acceptable to run the risk of ending the suffering patient's life. But, in saying this, they seem to be covertly signalling that poor-quality lives might be brought to an end – which they overtly want to avoid. Double effect, it seems, involves doublethink.

▶ Morphine, myths and motives

Given these criticisms, it is not surprising that some health-care professionals – and, indeed, some members of the public – feel uneasy about the principle and its use in terminal care. Are they right to be concerned?

Experts in palliative care say that there is little to fear, provided that the drugs are used appropriately. Their insights help to clarify some of the clinical confusion and, in turn, to refine our thinking about the philosophical principle.

The principle tends to be discussed when morphine or sedative drugs are considered. As well as relieving pain, such drugs can have significant side-effects, including sedation and the suppression of breathing. If, as a healthy adult, you were injected with a large dose of diamorphine or put into 'deep sedation' without any food or fluids, then the results could be catastrophic. But things might be very different for the dying patient whose symptoms needed to be addressed.

A terminally ill patient would be started on low doses, which might need to increase as symptoms worsen. The key is then to ensure that doses are adjusted, so that the beneficial effects outweigh any side-effects. Indeed, the evidence has long demonstrated that pain itself counteracts the risk of respiratory depression: with careful management of the drugs, the patient can be kept breathing, while their pain is reduced (Hanks and Twycross 1984).

Many studies have therefore shown that neither opioids nor sedatives necessarily pose a threat to continued life (Sykes and Thorns 2003). There may be the (very) limited case when double effect is needed, such as where the patient's breathing is already significantly compromised but they need relief from their distressing symptoms. But, overwhelmingly, the evidence shows that double effect is not needed at all, because the second effect (death) will have nothing to do with the drugs used – instead, the patient will have reached the natural end of his or her life, with their symptoms managed appropriately. Of course, the medication does indeed need to be managed appropriately if the potential lethal effects are to be avoided. Unfortunately, even many doctors remain confused about these drugs.

One study, from the UK, revealed that a third of non-specialists felt that their efforts to control symptoms had brought their patients' deaths forward by between a week and a month, and by up to a week in 60 per cent of cases (Seale 2006). But the question asked of them seemed to rest on the myth that morphine causes death, so the revelations are not that surprising.

Perhaps there are better ways of understanding such reports – that doctors are hastening their patients' deaths. We certainly need to distinguish between those who *use* the doctrine of double effect, those who are *confused* about it, and those who *misuse* it (Forbes and Huxtable 2006).

The first group of professionals, as we saw above, is likely to be small: it will encompass those caring for patients for whom relief might mean risk. The second group, sadly, seems to be much bigger. Specialists in palliative medicine know what they are doing (relieving symptoms, not killing), but too many others still think that opioids kill, when they usually do not. Little wonder, then, that the rest of us can be so confused (Reid, Gooberman-Hill and Hanks 2008). This is unfortunate because the risk now becomes that patients' pain will not be controlled when patients and doctors alike wrongly fear the use of powerful painkillers and other drugs used to control symptoms.

The third group of professionals, while probably also small, gives even more cause for concern. Misuse of the doctrine of double effect can run from euthanasia to something much more obviously sinister. So, a few doctors might say that they are seeking only to manage symptoms, when their real intentions are quite different.

Even Dr Adams was not all he appeared. Motive (and thus why one forms an intention) plays no direct part in the law of murder; intention (and thus what one was aiming at) is what counts for murder. The prosecutors will therefore seek to prove, on the balance of probabilities, that the accused's intention was to kill. The jury found that Adams's intention was innocent. Yet, after he died in 1983, Mr Hewitt, a Detective Chief Superintendent involved in the case, suggested that this was unlikely to have been the case.

Hewitt thought the prosecution had been bungled: Adams had actually inherited under 132 wills and, he implied, might even have murdered a potentially key prosecution witness. There are even suggestions that Adams was a role model for Harold Shipman, another GP, who was convicted in 2000 of murdering 15 patients, although he was suspected of killing many more (Huxtable 2007: 98). Shipman had given large doses of morphine to some patients whose deaths were not imminent and who had not previously received the drugs – with inevitable results.

Adams' motive therefore looked suspect and his resultant intention may have been far from innocent. Others who misuse the principle of double effect might have a more benign motivation. Remarkably, King George V's physician, Lord Dawson of Penn, admitted in his diary entry for 20 January 1936 that he had provided morphine and cocaine to the comatose and terminally ill monarch, in an attempt to 'determine the end' (Ramsay 1994). Lord Dawson described this as 'a facet of euthanasia or so-called mercy killing', although when the issue was debated in the House of Lords later that year, he spoke in opposition.

Of course, practitioners of euthanasia need not use painkilling drugs. In 1992 Dr Nigel Cox, a rheumatologist, was convicted of the attempted murder of Lillian Boyes, who repeatedly requested assisted dying as a release from the suffering associated with her rheumatoid arthritis (Huxtable 2007: 106–7). Cox used potassium chloride in a way that could only kill the patient (and not just the pain). As Mrs Boyes's body had been cremated, the prosecution could not prove beyond reasonable doubt that Cox had indeed killed the patient, so the charge of only attempted murder was brought – and found.

Although he was permitted to continue in practice, it is telling that Dr Cox was required to undergo further training in palliative care. The implication seems to be that there was more that could have been done for Mrs Boyes.

John Harris (1997: 36–40), a critic of double effect, thinks that its supporters focus too much on intention in a narrow sense, when really people should be held responsible for all that they achieve through their voluntary choices and actions. Harris has a point. But there must still be lines to be drawn between the different mental states that underlie particular actions. There is surely a world of difference between someone like Cicely Saunders, who intended to end pain (and that alone), someone like Nigel Cox, who appeared ignorant of the palliative options available, Lord Dawson, who apparently practised euthanasia, and Harold Shipman (or, for that matter, John Bodkin Adams), who was a serial killer.

So where are we left? Two renowned experts in end-of-life care, Rob George and Claud Regnard, provide a powerful summary:

> Double effect is relevant to every field of medicine and surgery, but only rarely to end-of-life care and it can never justify negligent or malicious practice.
>
> Double bind (that we can only treat pain, breathlessness and distress at the expense of shortening life) is factually wrong.
>
> Double jeopardy (that, since clinicians are willing to give medications despite the knowledge or belief that they may shorten life, means that they ought explicitly to end life in the suffering) is deceptive and unjustifiable. (George and Regnard 2007: 79)

These experts in palliative care think that assisted dying is unjustifiable. Others, like Dr Cox and Lord Dawson, might disagree. Let us turn to consider the main arguments given in favour of justifying – and legalizing – the practice.

8

For assisted dying

'"In 15 seconds you will receive a lethal injection and die. Do you wish to proceed? Yes or No?"'

ALL THAT MATTERS

Dogs do not have many advantages over people, but one of them is extremely important: euthanasia is not forbidden by law in their case; animals have the right to a merciful death. (Kundera 1999: 299)

Milan Kundera's observation in *The Unbearable Lightness of Being* generally holds true. In some countries, however, securing a merciful death for a fellow human is no longer forbidden by law. The first area in which this was explicitly allowed was the Northern Territory of Australia.

In that case: Bob Dent

On 22 September 1996 Bob Dent became the first person to die under a law permitting assisted dying. Three months earlier, the Rights of the Terminally Ill Act 1995 had come into force in the Northern Territory of Australia.

The Act applied only to those who were terminally ill and capable of making the choice to be assisted to die. If eligible, such a person could be assisted to die only by a doctor. Built into the legislative scheme were safeguards, including that the patient had had their condition and capacity confirmed by a second doctor and that there had been a 'cooling-off' period before euthanasia was performed.

Bob, a former pilot and carpenter, had prostate cancer, which had spread to his bone marrow. Taking 30 tablets a day and urinating through a catheter, he also had a recurring hernia and a collapsed lung. He decided that the time had come to put an end to his unwanted existence.

Having secured a favourable second opinion, Dr Philip Nitschke agreed to grant Bob's wish to die. Before doing so, he, Bob, and Bob's wife, Judy, shared a meal together. Dr Nitschke later reported that, while he was tense and Judy was upset, Bob was 'the happiest one of the lot of us'. After their meal, Bob said to the doctor: 'Let's get on with it. You're here to do a job.'

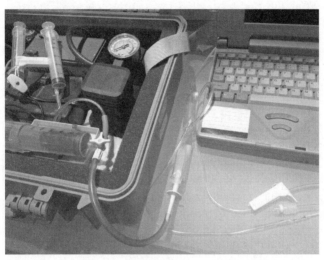

▲ Dr Nitschke's Deliverance Machine

Nitschke had with him the 'Deliverance Machine' (which is now on display in the Wellcome Collection, part of London's Science Museum). The device comprised a laptop computer, which was connected to a syringe driver, an intravenous drip and a lethal dose of barbiturates. This meant that Bob could follow the onscreen questions, until he reached the final screen, which asked: 'In 15 seconds you will receive a lethal injection and die. Do you wish to proceed? Yes or No?' Bob confirmed his wish; within a minute he was dead (Warne-Smith 2007).

Dr Nitschke assisted three more patients to die under this law, before it was overturned in 1997. Appalled at this reversal, Nitschke dubbed it a 'return to the jungle', when he spoke at a UK conference on euthanasia that year.

Although the Australian law lasted only nine months, other countries have since taken steps in the direction of legalizing assisted dying. The country with the longest history of permitting the practice is the Netherlands.

▶ Due care?

The Dutch debate on euthanasia was triggered by the Postma case in 1973, in which a doctor helped her dying mother to end her life, after clear and repeated requests for euthanasia (Rietjens et al. 2009). The doctor was convicted of murder but given only a short suspended sentence of imprisonment. In its judgement, the court indicated that there might be situations in which a doctor could help a suffering patient to die.

The criteria governing those situations in which euthanasia might be performed were developed over the next two decades, through further court cases and guidance issued by the Royal Dutch Medical Association. The criteria were made official on 1 April 2002, when the Euthanasia Act came into force. Euthanasia, as performed by a doctor, was to be permissible, provided that the following 'due care' criteria were satisfied:

▶ The patient's request is voluntary and well considered;

▶ The patient's suffering is unbearable and hopeless;

▶ The patient is informed about his or her situation and prospects;

▶ There are no reasonable alternatives;

▶ An independent physician is consulted; and

▶ The termination of life is performed with due medical care and attention (Rietjens et al. 2009).

Review committees exist to notify the prosecutor of any cases in which these conditions are not met.

The Netherlands' near neighbours have followed its lead, with Belgium and Luxembourg also recently enacting laws that permit voluntary euthanasia. There have also been developments farther away. In the United States, physician-assisted suicide (but not voluntary euthanasia) has been confirmed as lawful in Oregon, Washington and Montana, through either state legislation or the decision of a court.

Even countries that formally decline to allow such practices seem to recognize that assisted dying is rather different from other forms of homicide. In the UK, for example, judges tend to respond leniently to any 'mercy killer' who has sought to end the suffering of their loved one (Huxtable 2007), and prosecutors seem disinclined to take alleged instances of assisted suicide to court (Director of Public Prosecutions 2010).

The apparent softening of prosecution policy in England and Wales occurred in response to reports of terminally and critically ill people travelling to Switzerland, in order to receive assistance in suicide. These so-called 'suicide tourists' were usually helped to travel by family members, who were then at risk of prosecution back home for assisting the suicide – even though the suicide took place abroad. Switzerland was (and is) the destination because, like the old Northern Territory law but unlike those laws enacted elsewhere, assistance in suicide is available even to non-residents. Swiss law has no formal framework governing physician-assisted suicide: this can be provided by anyone, provided that they have no selfish motivation. The organization Dignitas has therefore helped people at home, as well as more than a hundred travellers from Britain, ranging from 23-year-old Daniel James to 85-year-old Sir Edward Downes, and even those from as far away as Australia (Huxtable 2009).

▶ Principled partings?

Advocates of assisted dying say it is not enough for the law to be lenient in application: it needs to be lenient in letter, too. Across the world, pressure seems to be growing for the policymakers to take something like the Dutch line. In England, for example, the Commission on Assisted Dying (2012) argued for the legalization of assisted dying.

That year Tony Nicklinson also tried – unsuccessfully – to persuade the courts of his right to die (Boseley 2012). Tony had 'locked-in syndrome', a condition powerfully described in Jean-Dominique Bauby's memoir *The Diving Bell and the Butterfly*. This is another of the 'disorders of consciousness' we encountered in Chapter 5, which 'results from brainstem pathology which disrupts the voluntary control of movement without abolishing either wakefulness or awareness. Patients who are "locked in" are substantially paralysed but conscious, and can communicate using movements of the eyes or eyelids' (Royal College of Physicians 2003).

Tony died only a few days after his arguments for assisted dying were rejected by the judges.

Beneath such arguments lie familiar positions on the value of life. Central to the advocates' cause is the self-determined value of life. As we saw in Chapter 1, Ronald Dworkin (1993: 217) thinks it 'a devastating, odious form of tyranny' to deny those – like Tony – who want the release that Australian Bob Dent sought and got.

Of course, the arguments for assisted dying do not only rest on what people want. Advocates also refer to what the terminally (or otherwise critically) ill need: a release from a life of suffering (De Haan 2002). The instrumental value of life therefore also plays its part in making the case for change.

▶ Cut out the claptrap?

The supporters think they have the moral high ground here. Echoing Kundera's point at the start of this chapter, Dr Nitschke says: 'It seems we demand humans to live with indignity, pain and anguish whereas we are kinder to our pets when their suffering becomes too much.

It simply is not logical or mature. Trouble is, we have had too many centuries of religious clap-trap' (quoted in Anon. 2009). Nitschke and his fellow supporters think that the intrinsic value of life should not constrain us all. As Bob Dent put it, in an open letter: 'If you don't agree with voluntary euthanasia, then don't use it, but don't deny me the right to use it if and when I want' (quoted in Warne-Smith 2007.)

As we saw in Chapter 6, the intrinsic value of life attitude does seem to have a great deal of work to do if it is to offer a convincing line between not doing everything to sustain every life, and not making those judgements about poor quality of lives that it so desperately seeks to avoid.

Advocates of assisted dying also reject the other arguments that are sometimes levelled at assisted dying. First, they say, it is offensive and wrong to suggest that there might be some benefit in struggling through one's final days. Similarly, the prospects of miracle cures or possible misdiagnoses being discovered should not be inflated.

Secondly, it seems we need not be unduly concerned about doctors getting involved in the 'killing business'. Medicine involves curing and caring – there need not be anything wrong in principle with it encompassing humanely practised assisted dying. Appeals to Hippocrates, with his central injunction 'First, do no harm', seem particularly misplaced here. Where is the 'harm', if the patient desperately wants to be released from life? Indeed, if one were sincerely to adhere to the Hippocratic principles of the Classical period, then our doctors would be required to pledge allegiance to a pantheon of ancient Greek gods (Gillon 1986: 226). Even if none of this convinces, then there is still the option of creating a brand-new specialist, like a 'thanatologist' (or 'death-bringer'), who need not be drawn from medicine's ranks (Brazier 1996).

Thirdly, supporters are critical of claims that allowing one form of assisted dying (like physician-assisted suicide) will lead, either in principle or in practice, to embracing other more questionable practices (like involuntary euthanasia). Some think the logic of the slippery slope simply doesn't work (Smith 2005). Others complain that such reasoning might be levelled at any attempt to try something new; if such warnings were heeded, then nothing would ever change.

Supporters of assisted dying suspect that, in truth, opponents fall back on these arguments in this context when really it is not only the bottom of the slope they fear, but also the top. In other words, opponents cry 'Slippery slope!' when a new step is envisaged, although really they oppose that first step – and probably because of their commitment to the intrinsic value of life (Doyal 2006).

Advocates think that their opponents are wrong, not only in opposing the first step but also in fearing a subsequent slide. The Netherlands, Oregon and elsewhere apparently demonstrate that safe systems can be created, and that boundaries between permissible and impermissible killings can be policed. Being open about such practices, they say, is surely better than leaving it to happen behind closed doors and without proper scrutiny (Magnusson 2002).

The analogies drawn by some opponents in an effort to evidence the slope in action also seem to be wrong-headed. Allowing abortion on request subject to certain criteria, as many countries do, does not seem to have signalled a general devaluing of human life or a slide into non-consensual terminations in those countries. And what the Nazis did, albeit in the name of 'euthanasia', is some significant distance from what advocates of assisted dying are talking about.

Equally, some of these objections can easily be turned against that which is already allowed. One can withdraw life-sustaining treatment for malevolent reasons, just as much as one can maliciously kill – but at least the former practice occurs openly, thus ensuring that some safeguards are in place to guard against ill will. One can also change one's mind about wanting to have treatment stopped, just as much as one might regret (in the brief moments left) a decision to be helped to die; in either case, it might be too late to go back. Indeed, many of life's decisions are irreversible, if only in the strict temporal sense. Unlike Marty McFly in the film *Back to the Future* (1985), we cannot jump back into the DeLorean, return to the past and make a different decision, which then adjusts our future life course.

The advocates of assisted dying seem to make a strong case for assisting someone like Bob Dent (whose case we considered at the beginning of this chapter) to die at a time and in a manner of his choosing. But are the opponents' arguments as flawed as these proponents insist? We shall see.

Against assisted dying

'If assisted dying is available, then what incentive do the doctors have for investing their time and energies in new ways to care and cure?'

ALL THAT MATTERS

Do not go gentle into that good night.
Rage, rage against the dying of the light.
(Thomas 2000)

Advocates of assisted dying promote 'gentle' exits for those who want to escape their suffering. But their opponents think, in the words of Dylan Thomas's celebrated poem, that we should 'rage against the dying of the light'. They point to various problems of principle and practice associated with assisted dying. Some of these difficulties emerge from a much-discussed case from the Netherlands, which involved a retired senator.

In that case: Edward Brongersma

In 2000, the Haarlem court considered the case of 86-year-old Edward Brongersma. Brongersma had first written a euthanasia declaration in 1984. He had informed his GP, Dr Philip Sutorius, of his wish to die on at least eight occasions.

Sutorius assisted Brongersma's suicide in 1998. A second doctor had confirmed that Brongersma had no psychiatric condition and that he was suffering unbearably. A month previously Brongersma had explained why he wanted to die: his existence was 'pointless and empty' and, while his loved ones had died, death had 'forgotten' him.

The prosecution sought a three-month suspended sentence for the GP, as it did not think that the 'unbearable suffering' requirement was satisfied. The court declined to penalize the doctor. Being 'tired of life', it seemed, could count for euthanasia. The Amsterdam Appeal Court, however, agreed with the prosecutor that this was too lenient. Sutorius was now convicted – but he was not sentenced to jail. Although he did not act for medical reasons, the court recognized Sutorius's compassionate motivation.

In 2002 the Dutch Supreme Court upheld the conviction. It insisted that the 'due care' criteria had to be followed – 'life fatigue' was not sufficient justification for assisted dying (Cohen-Almagor 2004: 164–7).

▶ Doctors' duties?

While they undoubtedly sympathize with the individuals' perceived predicaments, opponents of assisted dying insist that neither Edward Brongersma nor, indeed, Bob Dent should have had their requests granted. Their first line of opposition tends to be the intrinsic value of life. Believer and atheist alike essentially sign up to the first of the Ten Commandments: 'Do not kill' or, more accurately, 'Do not murder'.

Doctors, they say, should be particularly wedded to this ideal. As far back as Hippocrates, doctors – and their colleagues – have been healers, with special responsibilities for saving, prolonging and improving lives. While many of the Hippocratic traditions have been consigned to history, these core commitments remain. Notably, the first of the duties of a doctor listed by the UK General Medical Council (2013) is 'Make the care of your patient your first concern', while the last is 'Never abuse your patients' trust in you or the public's trust in the profession'. A commitment to patient welfare seems to underpin the trust that patients have in their carers. Wouldn't this be irreparably undermined if the carer were to become executioner?

This is not to say that medicine, or its practitioners, are perfect. Mistakes are made. But allowing euthanasia would itself appear to be a major mistake, given evidence of inaccurate diagnoses and prognoses. Indeed, one study has found that a number of patients diagnosed with terminal cancer not only did not have cancer, but were not terminally ill (Davis 1998: 21).

Mistakes like these are rare. But treatment will not always postpone the end, even for patients whose conditions have been correctly identified. Cures seldom appear overnight. But this does not mean that nothing can be done or that new treatments are not emerging. If assisted dying is available, then what incentive do the doctors have for investing their time and energies in new ways to care and cure?

There is already much that can be done for the dying patient, such that assisted dying is rarely (if ever) called for. The palliative care movement, pioneered by Dame Cicely Saunders in England, has spread throughout much of the developed world. Such holistic care at the end of life seems capable of tackling patients' symptoms and fears, thereby reducing requests for assisted dying. Dame Cicely herself said that only five of the 20,000 patients cared for in her hospice, St Christopher's in London, took their own lives, and that those who sought help in dying were 'almost always referring to previously unrelieved symptoms' (Saunders 1995: 44). Once the patient's symptoms were under control, then it seems they no longer sought assisted dying. Expert care can ease one's final days – and these are days that might offer valuable opportunities for reconciliations, realizations and the chance to say goodbye.

▲ Dame Cicely Saunders, pioneer of palliative care

Unfortunately, as we saw in Chapter 7, people appear to be confused about, or even unaware of, what palliative care can offer. Opinion polls often reveal significant support for assisted dying (House of Lords Select Committee 2005: 125–7). Public opinion is, of course, important in any democracy. But, to command respect, opinions need to be anchored in reality. How safe are such findings, when the questionnaires sometimes appear simplistic or confused, or are otherwise conducted when emotions are high, such as when the latest 'right to die' case has hit the headlines (Hagelin et al. 2004)?

▶ Slip-sliding away?

Opponents also dispute suggestions that euthanasia is safe and can be controlled. As we saw in Chapter 8, grim predictions are sometimes made about the slide down a slippery slope that will follow from even a seemingly modest and ethical proposal.

In 1958 Yale Kamisar, a law professor, advanced this argument in response to a leading criminal lawyer, Glanville Williams, who had argued in favour of voluntary euthanasia. Kamisar described himself as 'a non-Catholic and self-styled liberal'; his opposition was, he argued, founded on 'utilitarian ethics' (Kamisar 1958: 974). Utilitarians, you will recall, base morality on the outcomes of actions. Some utilitarians – like Peter Singer (1993) – argue that assisted dying can offer the best outcome for some patients. Kamisar suggests, however, that utilitarians need not be so accommodating, because the consequences can be bad.

One version of the 'thin end of the wedge' argument therefore points to the bad outcomes that are likely, in practice, to follow from adopting the proposal that is currently on the table. Some of these predictions and observations, for example around the perceived increase in abortions, seem inflated. But some evidence should cause us to pause.

Take the Netherlands, for example. The voluntary euthanasia policy adopted there was initially linked to the unbearable suffering associated with physical conditions, such as terminal illnesses. Yet, over time, its reach was extended. The first significant extension occurred when it was confirmed, in the wake of a legal case involving the assisted suicide of a depressed patient, that euthanasia could also be a legitimate response to psychiatric illness (*Office of Public Prosecutions v Chabot* (1994)). More recently, as we saw in Chapter 6, the Groningen protocol has allowed non-voluntary euthanasia for critically ill infants. Is it so unreasonable to suggest that the road to these developments was paved by the policy that was first adopted in the 1970s?

These extensions seem less surprising in the light of evidence that breaches of the 'due care criteria' (described in Chapter 8) do occur and that, when they do, the legal officials do not always take a dim view. Particularly troubling is the finding, in one of the annual reports of Dutch euthanasia statistics, that 1,000 (0.8 per cent) of the annual occurrences of euthanasia took place without any explicit request from the patient (Cohen-Almagor 2004: 75).

Leaving aside the Groningen protocol, euthanasia in the Netherlands must be voluntary if it is to be lawful. So these statistics clearly reveal that there was something unlawful going on. Maybe these patients were not killed against their will – perhaps the relevant forms were simply not completed correctly. But, if so, then one would still expect the Dutch legal system to punish such rule-breakers, so that the line between permissible and impermissible killings is held firm. Yet punishment does not necessarily follow – even Dr Sutorius did not serve prison time. Maybe, then, the Dutch have found themselves on the slippery slope that is feared by opponents of assisted dying. 'For inhabitants of such a flat country, the Dutch have proved remarkably fast skiers,' says John Keown (1997: 289).

Even if it were possible to put the brakes on the slide in practice, these might not withstand logical scrutiny. Proponents insist that the principles that justify assisted dying are safe and secure. The first of these is autonomy, according to which the value of life (and thus the decision to die) is a self-determined matter.

Some opponents believe that the proponents have misunderstood autonomy and its associated duties to safeguard others' freedoms. They add that autonomy should be a shield against unwanted bodily interference: it cannot be wielded as a sword to get what you want. And they further claim that, once we accept the case for allowing consensual assistance in dying when the person is suffering, we are logically required to go further.

According to this last argument, it is illogical to say that only assisted suicide, as performed by a physician, should be allowed on the basis of respecting autonomy. The same principle supports voluntary euthanasia, in which the doctor performs the final action, and even cases where it is not a doctor who is willing to help. Provided that the assistant is indeed willing, then their autonomy has also been respected, so there can be no complaint on the basis of autonomy. So the case of Dr Sutorius and Mr Brongersma cannot be ruled out in principle – even if the original proposal looks much more modest (like the Dutch one did) (Huxtable and Möller 2007).

We cannot even complain that there is no 'patient' as there is no underlying medical condition. Why do we even need a medical condition? If autonomy is our guide, then we need only two people who are willing to collaborate.

Of course, the case for euthanasia also rests on the obligation to remove suffering. Can this put the logical brakes on the slide down the slope? It seems not. For one thing, the obligation to eradicate suffering would appear to encourage the requirements to be softened. Why, for example, prolong the agony by insisting that there be a 'cooling-off' period between the patient's request and the performance of euthanasia (Kamisar 1958)?

We also cannot draw a logical line around which types of 'agony' will suffice to justify assisted dying. Consider again the Dutch move from physical illness, to psychiatric illness, to 'life fatigue'. There is nothing, in principle, to say that life fatigue does not involve great suffering. Suffering can arise from all manner of causes and take various forms, from acute pain to chronic distress.

The wide scope of 'suffering' seems to make a slide inevitable. Assume that I live in a country that permits assisted dying and that I have been diagnosed with early dementia. Euthanasia is scheduled because I want it, and you agree I should have it. Your agreement must mean that you share, or at least sympathize strongly with, my judgement on life with this condition, with all that it is likely to mean for my future. From agreeing to help me, to then helping a second patient with this condition, and then a third, isn't it likely that you will come to think that a life with Alzheimer's is a less than worthwhile life?

This sort of objection leads critics to argue that non-voluntary (and perhaps even involuntary) euthanasia follow on from voluntary euthanasia, because they are all based on the perceived poor quality of the patient's life. Most advocates of assisted dying tend to emphasize its voluntary versions. Len Doyal (2006) thinks this is because they stand the best chance of being legalized. But he believes a good case can also be made for non-voluntary euthanasia, for permanently incapacitated patients like Terri Schiavo (from Chapter 5). Groningen teaches us that these are not mere thought experiments. And isn't it telling that those who support such developments tend also to be the people who first wrote in support of voluntary euthanasia?

So how long might it be before someone seeks to defend involuntary euthanasia, in which there is no request or even consent from the patient? Such a practice is vividly depicted in the science-fiction novel and film *Logan's Run* (1976), in which death is mandatory at the age of 30. Of course, real support for involuntary euthanasia might seem unlikely because the practice looks so questionable – indeed, it looks like murder. But voluntary euthanasia was also once murder in those countries that have since allowed it.

We might wonder whether vulnerable patients are adequately protected in these countries. Can the safeguards deter unscrupulous doctors? Do they ensure that patients' requests are really free, and are not motivated by (say) a treatable depression or the feeling that they are a burden to their family or carers?

The very existence of the choice, in the law books, might be enough to put pressure on some patients (Velleman 1992).

So the critics say that assisted dying is not only wrong in principle but also too dangerous to contemplate. Humane support is what is needed, rather than risking the dehumanization that seems likely to follow from taking any steps in the direction of permission.

These arguments seem strong – but so did those in favour of assisted dying. Indeed, throughout this book we have encountered powerful appeals from different perspectives, whether we were talking about limiting treatment, relieving pain or directly ending life. So where does all this leave us? We will pick up this question in the final chapter.

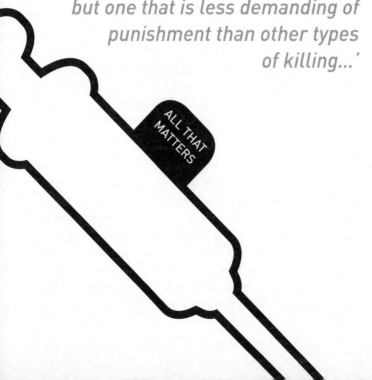

10

End matters

'Perhaps ... "euthanasia" or "mercy killing" should be given a special legal status, which keeps it a crime, but one that is less demanding of punishment than other types of killing...'

ALL THAT MATTERS

Maybe ... yes or no life-and-death decisions are easier to make because they are so black and white. I can cope with them because it's easier. Human emotions, well ... they're just a fathomless collection of greys and I don't do so well on the midtones. (Fforde 2001: 355)

So says Thursday Next, the central character in Jasper Fforde's comic fantasy novels. But, unlike Thursday, you may have found that the blacks and whites associated with life-and-death decisions have merged into 'a fathomless collection of greys' as this book has progressed. So where are we left?

▶ 50 shades of grey?

We have considered three different ways of thinking about the value of life: one emphasizes the value of life itself, and thus the obligation to avoid killing, another prefers to see life in terms of its quality, such that some poor-quality lives might be ended early, while the third leaves any final decision to individual choice.

There is much to commend in each of these perspectives. Human life surely merits special concern and protection; suffering should be brought to an end wherever possible; and only tyrants will ignore what people want. It is not surprising, then, that each of these viewpoints commands a great deal of support and that, despite centuries (and more) of debate and disagreement, no single position has managed to defeat its rivals.

Sometimes one particular approach will appear stronger than the others. But appearances can also be deceptive. Ms B's right to decline life-saving treatment seemed unassailable. And yet the underlying principle, respect for autonomy, encountered difficulties when it was extended to patients who no longer had the capacity to decide at the critical time, like Mrs Malette. Many people simply don't make their wishes known in advance; relatives can provide some help here, but how sure can we be that they are honouring what the patient would want? And what if the patient is an infant, who has never held any views on anything? Even if we do know what the patient wants because they have the relevant capacity to decide, here and now, we might still wonder how far the idea should be taken. Bob Dent seemed to have a good case for claiming a right to be assisted to die – but did Edward Brongersma?

Similar things might be said in relation to the intrinsic value of life. If any society is to exist and flourish, something like a law of murder looks essential, with its insistence that death should not be caused intentionally. Yet problems arise when we try to give meaning to concepts like 'intention' and 'causation'. Does foreseeing death as a result of palliative medication amount to 'intending' that death? Do omissions 'cause' death in a morally relevant (or problematic) sense? Is there such a thing as 'passive euthanasia'? Cases like those of Charlotte Wyatt and the potholer (in Chapter 7) point to the fine lines that are sometimes drawn around 'disproportionate' treatments, 'intentions' and the like, which threaten to take the intrinsic value-of-life approach into territory it wants to avoid.

In this territory, quality-of-life considerations dictate who should live and who should die. There may be something to be said for this, such as when a decision is made to remove life-sustaining treatment from a patient like Terri Schiavo or when conjoined twins like Gracie and Rosie are separated so that one may be given the chance of life. But how far ought such logic to be extended? Is, for example, the Groningen protocol, authorizing non-voluntary euthanasia for critically ill infants, a welcome development?

Anna's story, in the first chapter, seemed to involve all of these issues and principles. As we have traced the principles, we have seen problems with them all. As the label implies, the sanctity of life seems to carry a great deal of religious baggage; the instrumental value of life raises the spectre of eugenics; and self-determination threatens to turn into a free-for-all of claim and counter-claim, in which anything goes (provided I want it enough).

Occasionally, the conflicts between these positions will be all too vivid. Abortion providers in the United States have been bombed and shot at by pro-life opponents. Violence has also been encountered by those who deal with the issues at the other of life, on which we have focused: Peter Singer, who supports euthanasia, has written about being assaulted when lecturing on his ideas in Germany; Dr Nigel Cox received death threats from someone who felt he had been treated too leniently by the legal and medical authorities; and family members have even assaulted doctors on the wards who they (wrongly) thought were seeking to euthanize a young patient (Huxtable 2007: 30).

Such extreme reactions, while rare, are undeniably questionable. Yet even when the disputes are confined to the newspapers and professional journals, advocates of the different positions insist that they are right – and that their opponents must be wrong. I suspect that the issues are not so black and white; indeed, I think there are fifty (or more) shades of grey here.

My own views have evolved over the years, and may well do so again. Mindful of the problems of meaning, scope and appeal to which I referred in Chapter 1, I currently think there is a good case for thinking about compromise in relation to these disputed matters of life and death. My reasons for thinking so are as follows:

▶ *Uncertainty and complexity.* Everywhere we have looked in these debates, there was major uncertainty and complexity. Morally, we cannot agree on the best guiding principle (or principles); indeed, we cannot even agree about the subjects of moral concern, when we think back to the problems associated with 'personhood'. Add to these concerns the considerable scientific questions: Is the apparently unconscious patient indeed unconscious? When can we be sufficiently certain that the prospects are so bleak that treatment should be avoided, given that a patient like Charlotte Wyatt appeared, against expectations, to thrive?

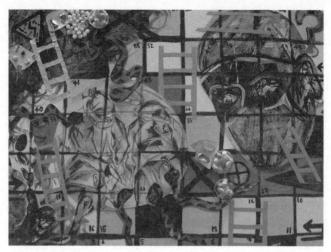

▲ Onwards or backwards? Decision-making at the end of life is rife with uncertainty and complexity.

▌ *Relationships must continue.* Ways forward are needed that enable people to continue to coexist peacefully. Relationships must endure – whether these be between patients, loved ones and professionals who might disagree, or between citizens at large, who cling to a vast plurality of beliefs even within one society.

▌ *We cannot honour every competing value, but each value should be represented.* Sometimes, as we have seen, it seems impossible that a decision can respect two (or more) principles that pull in different directions. And yet we still need the advocates of the different principles to put their cases as strongly as possible; if they fail to do so, they can only lose out, and there is the risk that the wrong approach will come to dominate.

▶ *Decisions are needed.* In many of the situations we have considered, we cannot leave these debates to the ivory towers of academia – decisions are needed in the real world.

As these conditions seem to be present in so many of the situations we have considered, isn't there a case for compromise at the end of life?

▶ Deciding together

So what might a compromise policy on end-of-life decision-making look like? Before his attention turned to the No. 1 Ladies' Detective Agency, Alexander McCall Smith was an academic medical lawyer in Scotland. He had the following to say:

> *Moral debates of the sort surrounding euthanasia involve the engagement of frequently very different visions of human goods... Of course the euthanasia debate will rumble on... but the defence of the middle ground, currently occupied by English law, is a worthwhile enterprise. In this particular debate, there are worse places to be.* (McCall Smith 1999: 207)

English law certainly seems to occupy the middle ground: although it does not openly endorse active euthanasia or assisted suicide, its legal officials appear to respond leniently when these occur, and the law also allows for treatment to be refused, life support to be withdrawn from incapacitated patients, and potentially lethal drugs to be given to manage symptoms.

If the middle ground is the right place to be, then maybe the law in England – and also in other countries, like Germany, that seem to take similar approaches – can go further. Perhaps, for example, 'euthanasia' or 'mercy killing' should be given a special legal status, which keeps it a crime, but one that is less demanding of punishment than other types of killing (Huxtable 2007: 165–71). For those who are convicted, the penalty could take the form of counselling or further training (such as in palliative care), rather than imprisonment. This would seem to split the difference between arguments for and against the practice. Those opposed can still point to the crime, while those in favour will see the legal position somewhat softened in recognition of their moral arguments.

Of course, each side will still have cause to complain, either because the proposal goes too far, or because it does not go far enough. But that would seem to signal that a compromise has indeed been reached: in a compromise, one makes gains and incurs losses.

This example will still be controversial for some. Indeed, finding the middle ground is rarely straightforward. Fundamentally, it depends on *negotiation* and, therefore, discussion.

Discussion might lead to agreement and consensus, or it might open up new alternatives, which manage to accommodate arguments on either side. If the course chosen is to be appropriately principled, then certain ground rules will still need to be observed (Huxtable 2012). Those speaking will need to make their cases in *reliable* ways, not misrepresenting or over-claiming in the hope of gaining more at the end. The different opponents will also need to be appropriately *respectful* of one another, letting others make their case and accepting that their rivals will also have good reasons for making that case. Of course, quite how good these reasons are should also be open to challenge – cases therefore need to be made in the most *reflective* and critically robust ways. Writing as the Second World War began, T.V. Smith suggested that it is the politician's job

> to find a middle course between two sincere and tangible positions. To locate the middle ground they must reckon from stationary banks. If you do not insist upon your cause, they will have to deal with shifting banks as well as the whirling currents of conflict in their efforts to locate the middle of the stream. (Smith 1942: 13)

These discussions of conflicting views might occur nationally or locally. Nationally, legislatures, the courts and even (as, for example, in Belgium, France and Singapore) a bioethics commission might be expected to discuss the issues. We all have the right – and probably also the obligation – to contribute to these discussions, as they concern matters that, in one way or another, are likely to affect us all. Keep an eye out for such opportunities: they might involve government consultations on proposed changes to the law, giving evidence or providing opinions to commissions and pollsters, or simply voting for candidates in elections. And if, as we saw in Chapter 9, the questions posed are based on shaky assumptions, then take the opportunity to point this out, so that the debate can be as informed as possible.

Attempts to resolve ethical dilemmas can also arise at the local level, whether in discussions between clinicians, patients and the family, or (as we saw in Chapter 5) in clinical ethics committees.

Of course, open discussion will not always mean that a consensus or compromise can be reached. Sometimes an outside decision-maker, such as a judge, will be needed to give the last word. The problem with many legal systems is that they are adversarial in nature, and they therefore tend to transform the parties into 'winner' and 'loser'. Whether this is the right way of approaching cases like Terri Schiavo's, for example, is open to question. As Charlotte Wyatt's case (which went to court at least 11 times) shows, the court might not always be the best place to reach compromises that are sensitive to the arguments on both sides. Ethics committees and mediators might therefore also be called on, where they are available, so that the proper emphasis is placed on discussion and negotiation.

▶ At the end

Open discussion, then, seems to offer a way forward. Only through this might we test our arguments, beliefs and principles, with a view to ensuring that we promote and follow the most appropriate course. Indeed, Anna – whose story opened this book – encouraged such debate, when she asked that her story be discussed after her death.

Having read this book, you may have had your own previous views affirmed. But I hope that there will also have been occasions when your views were tested – with the result that they were abandoned, if necessary, or otherwise amended, so as to become as cogent as possible.

I therefore hope that this book has helped you to prepare for any future discussions you might have about your own care or that of your family or friends. As the Dying Matters coalition puts it: 'Dying matters – let's talk about it.'

This 100 Ideas section gives ways you can explore the subject in more depth. It's much more than just the usual reading list.

Ten patients

1   **Ms B** had life-supporting treatment withdrawn at her request in 2002, after she took her case to court in England. Failure to honour Ms B's decision, which she was competent to make, meant the doctors had 'trespassed' against her person.

2   **Anthony Bland** was trapped in the crush at the Hillsborough Stadium disaster of 1989 in Sheffield in the UK. He was later diagnosed as being in a persistent vegetative state, and life-sustaining nutrition and hydration were withdrawn following a landmark ruling in 1993, which had the backing of his family and doctors. The judges ruled that removing such support was not murder because this was in Tony's 'best interests', so there was no duty to continue with treatment.

3   **Bob Dent** was the first person ever to receive assistance in dying lawfully, under a law enacted in the Northern Territory of Australia in 1995. The law lasted only nine months before it was overturned. Although it has a longer history of permitting the practice, it was not until 2002 that the Netherlands formalized its position on voluntary euthanasia.

4   **Eluana Englaro,** from Italy, who was in a vegetative state, had life-supporting treatment withdrawn in 2009, following a hotly contested legal case that lasted two decades, in which even the Prime Minister, Silvio Berlusconi, became involved.

5   **Jean Humphry** was the wife of British journalist Derek Humphry. Following his wife's assisted death, which he described in the book *Jean's Way: A Love Story* (1978), Humphry became a prominent advocate of assisted dying, campaigning particularly in the United States. Humphry founded the Hemlock Society in 1980 and went on to write *Final Exit: The Practicalities of Self-Deliverance and Assisted Suicide for the Dying* (1992), which controversially provided advice on methods of 'self-deliverance'.

6   **Daniel James** was a young rugby player who was paralysed by an accident during training. In 2008 Daniel travelled from England to Switzerland, where he was assisted in his suicide by the organization Dignitas.

7   **Dianne Pretty,** who had the degenerative disorder motor neurone disease (also known as amyotrophic lateral sclerosis), petitioned the English courts and the European Court of Human Rights in Strasbourg for a change in the law to allow assisted suicide, so that her husband, Brian, could help her to die. She died of natural causes in 2002, after her final appeal failed to find favour among the judges.

8   Karen Ann Quinlan was the first patient in a persistent vegetative state from whom life-supporting ventilation was withdrawn, following a 1976 court ruling in the United States. When treatment was withdrawn, Karen proved able to breathe unassisted; given tube-feeding, she lived until 1985, when her death followed complications from pneumonia.

9   Sue Rodriguez was a Canadian woman with motor neurone disease who failed to persuade the Canadian courts, in 1993, that she should have a legal right to be assisted in her suicide. Sue's suicide was subsequently aided by a doctor, whose identity was never revealed.

10 Terri Schiavo, from Florida, USA, was in a vegetative state for many years before life-sustaining nutrition and hydration were withdrawn from her in 2005. Withdrawal followed an intense and protracted legal battle between members of her family, in which (in a similar way to Eluana Englaro's case) the American President became embroiled.

Ten doctors

11 John Bodkin Adams was a GP in England who was acquitted, in 1957, of murdering his patient Edith Morrell using morphine. However, later evidence – including that the doctor had inherited under many patients' wills – suggests that his actions might not have been so innocent.

12 Boudewijn Chabot was a Dutch psychiatrist who, in 1991, helped a seriously depressed (but otherwise physically well) patient to die.

13 Nigel Cox was a rheumatologist in England who was convicted, in 1992, of attempting to murder a patient, Lillian Boyes, at her request. Cox did not serve time in

prison and was allowed to continue in practice, but he was required to undergo further training in palliative care.

14 **Ilora Finlay** is a consultant in palliative medicine based in Wales, who is also a member of the House of Lords and has served on a Parliamentary Select Committee that explored – but rejected – the possibility of relaxing the law in England and Wales on assisted dying.

15 **Michael Irwin** is a former doctor in England who has claimed to have helped patients to die and has long campaigned for a change in the law.

16 **Jack Kevorkian** was an American doctor who helped patients to commit suicide across the United States. After many trials, he was ultimately found guilty of breaking the criminal law.

17 **Elisabeth Kübler-Ross** was a Swiss-American psychiatrist who famously identified five stages of grief that might be experienced by the terminally ill or their grieving loved ones, in her book *On Death and Dying* (1969). The five stages, which she acknowledged were not necessarily complete or chronological, are: denial, anger, bargaining, depression and acceptance.

18 **Cicely Saunders** was a pioneer of hospice and palliative care who set up St Christopher's Hospice in London.

19 **Harold Shipman** was a doctor and a notorious English serial killer, whose actions, while scarcely resembling assisted dying, have cast a long shadow over the law in this area.

20 **Anne Turner** was a British GP who, after being diagnosed with the progressive and incurable degenerative disease supranuclear palsy, travelled to Switzerland in 2006 for assistance in suicide. The BBC dramatized her story in 2009 in *A Short Stay in Switzerland.*

Ten places

21 Belgium. The termination of life on request is permitted, under a law passed in 2002.

22 Germany. Euthanasia is not allowed and the term itself tends not to be used, although debates about legalizing assisted suicide continue.

23 India. In 2011 the Supreme Court of India set down the conditions in which life-sustaining treatment might be withdrawn from patients in the permanent vegetative state. Active euthanasia would remain unlawful but treatment might be stopped, provided that the court agreed. In the ensuing debates, concerns were expressed about the weak rule of law in India, the gap between rich and poor, and the risk of abuse. Reports suggest that many in India's majority Hindu culture feel that euthanasia interferes with the reincarnation cycle and thus trespasses against the divine.

24 Italy. Although there has been a lively debate following widely publicized cases, legal and medical authorities remain firmly opposed to euthanasia in this predominantly Roman Catholic country.

25 Luxembourg. Assisted suicide and voluntary euthanasia were legalized in 2009.

26 The Netherlands. Dutch law has evolved since the 1970s and is now clearly stated in an Act according to which voluntary euthanasia and assisted suicide are allowed, provided that the specified 'due care' criteria are satisfied. Controversially, a protocol adopted in Groningen has also allowed non-voluntary euthanasia of critically ill infants, provided that their parents consent.

27 The Northern Territory of Australia. Voluntary euthanasia was lawful for almost a year in the late 1990s.

28 **Oregon, USA.** Oregon legalized assisted suicide in 1994 in the Death with Dignity Act. Washington adopted a similar law in 1998, while Montana legalized the practice in 2009, following a court decision. Elsewhere in the United States, the practice remains illegal.

29 **Switzerland.** Assisted suicide is not a crime unless the assistant had a 'selfish motive' for acting (such as an expected financial reward). There are no official criteria governing assisted suicide in Switzerland, although organizations like EXIT-Deutsche and Dignitas have their own procedures. Dignitas has even been willing to help those coming from outside Switzerland, in what has become known as 'suicide tourism'.

30 **The UK.** Neither euthanasia nor assisted suicide is lawful, but prosecution policy in England and Wales is relatively lenient in relation to assisted suicide. Remarkably, Scottish law seems to lack the specific crime of assisting in suicide, although such an action might amount to a crime like culpable homicide.

Five misconceptions

31 **Patients from whom life-sustaining treatment is withdrawn will endure prolonged and painful deaths.** This is not the case. A decision to stop providing life support is, of course, not taken lightly: it usually follows careful discussion within the medical team and with the patient (where possible), his or her family, and sometimes also an ethics committee or a judge. When the health-care team has resolved to remove a ventilator or, say, the tubes delivering nutrition and hydration, efforts will then be made to ensure that the patient is comfortable during the dying process, through the provision of pain-relieving drugs and, sometimes, sedatives.

32 **Strong painkillers (like morphine) and sedative drugs are likely to shorten life when they are used in high doses to treat a patient who is already dying.** This is untrue – in fact, the evidence suggests that, when they are given by skilled experts, these drugs have no effect on when the patient dies. One study even found that the patients receiving these strong drugs actually survived for longer than they would have been expected to do so if they had not been so treated.

33 **Terminally ill patients who request euthanasia or assisted suicide want an escape from their pain.** Certainly, some such requests are so motivated, but research reveals that more often it is the loss of autonomy that people want to avoid. Indeed, in countries where assisted dying is lawful, there is a marked difference between the number of people initially requesting help in dying and the number of those who ultimately decide to take up the option.

34 **Euthanasia is what the Nazis did.** This is an inaccurate and unfair argument against permitting euthanasia because the sorts of proposals promoted nowadays – which focus on the suffering of terminally ill patients and the desire, among some such patients, for an easeful passing – are some considerable distance from the murderous campaigns of the Third Reich. Of course, there is plenty of scope to argue about the ethics of euthanasia (as understood in the modern sense), but it is plainly wrong to believe that these discussions bear any resemblance to what Hitler was doing.

35 **The law can either allow assisted dying or it cannot – there is no middle ground.** Amid all the talk of whether or not the law should be reformed through the legalization or decriminalization of assisted dying, the point is sometimes lost that, in truth, the law is rarely a blunt instrument where euthanasia is concerned. Stern prohibitions on intentional killing do not always translate into harsh penalties. Relatives who have acted on the pleas of their loved one and doctors who have sought to end their patient's misery have seldom faced the full force of the criminal law; instead, lenient sentences are passed (often with no prison time) and ways are found of counselling – and, in the case of some doctors, retraining – the perpetrator.

Ten films

36 *Dark Victory* (1939). Bette Davis stars as a socialite who is diagnosed with a brain tumour. Directed by Edmund Goulding, the film also stars Humphrey Bogart and a pre-presidential Ronald Reagan.

37 *It's a Wonderful Life* (1946). James Stewart stars in this classic, directed by Frank Capra, about a man contemplating suicide.

38 *Logan's Run* (1976). Michael York and Jenny Agutter lead this film, directed by Michael Anderson, about a future society in which everyone must die on reaching the age of 30.

39 *Whose Life Is It Anyway?* (1981). Featuring Richard Dreyfuss and John Cassavetes, and directed by John Badham, this film – based on Brian Clark's popular play – tells the story of an artist's fight for his life support to be removed.

40 *My Life* (1993). After he relinquished Batman's cape and cowl, Michael Keaton played a terminally ill man who prepared for his death by video-recording his final months for his wife, played by Nicole Kidman, who is pregnant with their first child. Directed by Bruce Joel Rubin.

41 *The English Patient* (1996). Anthony Minghella directed Ralph Fiennes, Kristin Scott Thomas and Juliette Binoche in this Oscar-winning version of Michael Ondaatje's novel about a burned pilot who is being nursed at the close of the Second World War.

42 *Talk to Her* [*Hable con Ella*] (2002). This Spanish film, directed by Pedro Almodóvar, and featuring Javier Cámara, Leonor Watling, Darío Grandinetti and Rosario Flores, depicts the friendship that develops between two men, both of whom are caring for comatose women.

43 *The Sea Inside* [*Mar Adentro*] (2004). Directed by Alejandro Amenábar and starring Javier Bardem, this award-winning film, also from Spain, tells the story of Ramón Sampedro, whose plea for assisted suicide came before – but was ultimately rejected by – the European Commission on Human Rights.

44 *Million Dollar Baby* (2004). This is another award-winning film, this time directed by Clint Eastwood, who also stars, alongside Hilary Swank and Morgan Freeman. Ostensibly the tale of a boxer (spoiler alert!), the film comes to deal with some of the issues raised in this book.

45 *You Don't Know Jack* (2010). An HBO TV movie, starring Al Pacino as notorious Dr Jack Kevorkian, about how his provision of assistance in suicide led to him coming before the US Supreme Court.

Fifteen concepts

46 **Advance directives,** sometimes known as 'living wills' (or even 'Ulysses contracts'), involve specifying your wishes about what treatment you want – or, particularly, do not want – in the event of you becoming incapable of making a decision at the critical time.

47 **Assisted suicide** is where the person who has chosen to die performs the final act, having been helped in some way by another. This other person might be a doctor who has provided the pills (hence *physician-assisted suicide*).

48 **Autonomy** means 'self-rule'. The principle of respect for autonomy means honouring those choices made by people who have the relevant capacity to decide, and who have done so freely and with sufficient information.

49 **Cardiopulmonary resuscitation** (CPR) involves attempting to restore some of the flow of oxygenated blood to the brain and heart, following cardiac arrest (heart attack). Although sometimes depicted as inevitably successful in television dramas, modern guidance talks of '(not) *attempting* resuscitation'. This helps to convey the reality that, despite their best efforts, professionals will not always be able to bring the patient back. Indeed, it can be inappropriate to do so, especially if the heart stops as part of the natural dying process.

50 **Competence** refers to the specific capacity needed to make a decision. Central to such capacity will be the ability to receive and retain information, which is then used to reach and communicate a decision.

51 **Death with dignity** can be a slippery notion, which has been used as a rallying cry both by those who take a 'pro-life' position and those who adopt a 'pro-choice' position on assisted dying. For those opposed to the practice, dignity reflects the sanctity of human life; for those in favour, dignity involves respecting autonomous choices (including a choice to die).

52 **Euthanasia,** literally a 'good death', nowadays refers to the intentional ending of a life of suffering. The term tends to be reserved for situations involving doctors, as is also often the case with the phrase *assisted dying*. Euthanasia can take a variety of forms, depending on whether the patient is capable of requesting this and does indeed do so (in which case it is voluntary, as opposed to involuntary or non-voluntary), and whether it is achieved by action or omission (and so is active or passive). When relatives or other loved ones are involved, then the term *mercy killing* tends to be applied.

53 **Futility** is another slippery concept, which tends to signal that life-sustaining treatment should not be attempted or continued because it will not have the desired effect. Questions linger over what the desired effect should be (sustaining the body as a machine or offering hope to patients and families?) and when, if ever, the label should be applied.

54 **Human rights** tend to be expressed in law, whether nationally or internationally, and they place corresponding duties on others not to interfere with those rights. Such rights include the right to life, the right to privacy and self-determination, and the right to be free from unjust discrimination. Where assisted dying is concerned, different rights (and duties) appear to come into conflict.

55 **Lasting power of attorney.** This is the concept used in the law of England and Wales but other countries talk of *proxies* and *surrogate decision-making.* The basic idea is the same: before losing the capacity to decide, someone can appoint another person (a proxy) to take critical decisions for them in the event of them losing capacity.

56 **Personhood** is yet another complicated idea. It can refer to the subject of moral concern: 'persons' are those who, for example, are capable of valuing their own existence. Such individuals might be said to have *rights* and the like; those who lack the characteristics necessary for personhood (such as embryos and neonates) might still have some *interests*, but some philosophers claim that they are not due the more significant entitlements that are owed to full moral agents (persons). Personhood can also be an issue in another sense, in terms of personal identity. Questions therefore sometimes arise about whether the individual who has lost capacity is still the same individual as the competent person they were previously.

57 **Quality of life** involves a relative judgement, for example, between a person's previous and current existence or between that person's life and the lives of others. Health care is undeniably concerned with improving the quality of patients' lives. However, some philosophers seek to take the idea further than many health-care professionals would like, by arguing that poor-quality lives can be ended – in other words, that euthanasia can be acceptable.

58 **Sanctity of life** is a religious idea that recognizes the intrinsic value of human life, such that it should never intentionally be brought to a premature end. Similar ideas are sometimes expressed in the more secular terms of the 'right to life'.

59 **Slippery slope** arguments are those that claim that permitting one (innocent) practice will lead, either in practice or in principle, to more questionable practices. Arguments rage about whether such claims are logical or plausible.

60 **Suicide** involves intentionally ending one's own life. Whether a death might be classified as suicide can be a sensitive and disputed matter. In *Suicide* (1897), Emile Durkheim, a French sociologist, suggested that 'suicide' applies 'to all cases of death resulting directly or indirectly from a positive or negative act of the victim himself, which he *knows will produce this result*'. For some, this casts the net too wide. Is, for example, a Jehovah's Witness who declines a life-saving blood transfusion thereby committing suicide?

Five distinctions

61 Acting and omitting. A distinction is sometimes drawn between acting and omitting, which might also be described in terms of doing and allowing, acting and refraining, and (active) euthanasia as opposed to withholding or withdrawing treatment. Actions, it is thought, are worse than omissions, even if the omissions have the same effect as the actions. Critics dispute the distinction, particularly when it is used to permit the removal of life-supporting treatment from a patient who (they argue) might benefit more from a humane lethal injection.

62 Assisted suicide and voluntary euthanasia. Assisted suicide tends to involve the suffering person taking the final, lethal step. With euthanasia, meanwhile, the final step is performed by another person, such as a doctor. Some claim that assisted suicide offers the more obvious expression of autonomy, although voluntary euthanasia also appeals to the same principle.

63 Intention and foresight. The doctrine of double effect seeks to distinguish between intending a prohibited result and merely foreseeing such a result as an incidental effect of acting with a good intention. The principle tends to be applied to the use of powerful painkillers in end-of-life care, although there is evidence to suggest that professionals who use such drugs appropriately have little to fear in terms of the secondary effect.

64 Proportionate and disproportionate treatments. Advocates of the intrinsic value of life sometimes point to a distinction between proportionate (or ordinary) and disproportionate (or extraordinary) responses to a patient's plight. Disproportionate responses are not required, such as when the burdens associated with treatment outweigh its benefits, or treatment is considered to be futile; proportionate responses, however, are required, such as when the anticipated benefits of treatment clearly outweigh any costs.

65 Outcomes, duties and characters. Ethical theory tends to be concerned with two questions: How should I act? And who should I be? Those interested in the first question often judge actions in terms of either their outcomes (which form the main focus for consequentialists, such as utilitarians) or the duties that a moral agent is obliged to act on (which is the central issue for deontologists). Those interested in the second question tend instead to emphasize character and thus the acquisition of virtues and the avoidance of vices (as in virtue ethics).

Five remarkable facts

66 Deliverance on the high seas? The 'Deliverance Machine' used by Dr Philip Nitschke in the Northern Territory of Australia, when assisted dying was lawful there, was bought by the Science Museum in London. It is exhibited in the Wellcome Collection. Since the law was overturned, Nitschke has campaigned for assisted dying. He once considered taking his campaign to the seas: he contemplated launching a 'euthanasia ship', which would have been registered in the Netherlands (where euthanasia has long been allowed).

67 Artists and anguish? In his widely known comic strip *The Far Side*, Gary Lawson includes a cartoon featuring Jack Kevorkian, in which the doctor realizes that his girlfriend is also dating the Grim Reaper. Kevorkian himself was something of an artist – search the Web for examples of some of his rather remarkable paintings. Not for the faint-hearted.

68 Guilty of assisting an innocent act? Suicide is not unlawful in England and Wales, although assisted suicide is.

Suicide was decriminalized so as to remove the threat of a criminal trial from those who had failed in their attempts (such people were at risk of prosecution for the crime of attempted suicide). Sympathy and support, rather than prosecution, was understandably thought to be the more humane response to such individuals. Despite the change in the law, it is notable that we continue to talk of 'committing' suicide, as if the practice was still unlawful.

69 Discworld, dementia and assisted dying? Sir Terry Pratchett, award-winning author of the Discworld fantasy books, was diagnosed with early-onset Alzheimer's disease in 2007, since when he has spoken of his support for assisted suicide. He also provided funding for a Commission on Assisted Dying in England, which was chaired by Lord Falconer. The Commission recommended in 2012 that the law be amended to allow assisted dying.

70 The birth of a good death? The Roman historian Suetonius (c.70–140 CE), in *The Lives of the Caesars*, was apparently the first to use the term 'euthanasia', when he described how the Emperor Augustus, 'dying quickly and without suffering in the arms of his wife, Livia, experienced the "euthanasia" he had wished for'.

Ten websites

71 Age UK: http://www.ageuk.org.uk/

72 British Medical Association: http://www.bma.org.uk/

73 Dignitas: http://www.dignitas.ch/

74 Dignity in Dying: http://www.dignityindying.org.uk/

75 European Association for Palliative Care: http://www.eapcnet.eu/

76 Euthanasia.com: http://www.euthanasia.com/

77 General Medical Council: http://www.gmc-uk.org/

78 National Council for Palliative Care:
http://www.ncpc.org.uk/

79 St Christopher's Hospice:
http://www.stchristophers.org.uk/

80 World Federation of Right to Die Societies:
http://www.worldrtd.net/

Twenty further reading suggestions

81 Margaret Battin, *Ending Life: Ethics and the Way We Die*
(Oxford: OUP, 2005)

82 Martin Benjamin, *Philosophy and this Actual World*
(Lanham, MD: Rowman and Littlefield, 2003)

83 Nigel Biggar, *Aiming to Kill: The Ethics of Suicide and
Euthanasia* (London: Darton, Longman & Todd, 2003)

84 Donna Dickenson, Richard Huxtable and Michael Parker,
The Cambridge Medical Ethics Workbook (Cambridge:
Cambridge University Press, 2nd edition, 2010)

85 Gerald Dworkin, R.G. Frey and Sissela Bok, *Euthanasia
and Assisted Suicide: For and Against* (Cambridge:
Cambridge University Press, 1998)

86 Ronald Dworkin, *Life's Dominion: An Argument about
Abortion and Euthanasia* (London: HarperCollins, 1993)

87 Jonathan Glover, *Causing Death and Saving Lives* (London:
Penguin Books, 1977)

88 John Griffiths, Heleen Weyers and Maurice Adams,
Euthanasia and Law in Europe (Oxford: Hart Publishing,
2008)

89   John Harris, *The Value of Life: An Introduction to Medical Ethics* (London: Routledge and Kegan Paul, 1985)

90   Richard Huxtable, *Euthanasia, Ethics and the Law: From Conflict to Compromise* (London: Routledge-Cavendish, 2007)

91   Richard Huxtable, *Law, Ethics and Compromise at the Limits of Life: To Treat or Not to Treat?* (London: Routledge, 2012)

92   Emily Jackson and John Keown, *Debating Euthanasia* (London: Hart, 2011)

93   David Jeffrey, *Against Physician Assisted Suicide: A Palliative Care Perspective* (Oxford: Radcliffe, 2009)

94   John Keown (ed.), *Euthanasia Examined: Ethical, Clinical and Legal Perspectives* (Cambridge: Cambridge University Press, 1997)

95   John Keown, *Euthanasia, Ethics and Public Policy: An Argument Against Legalisation* (Cambridge: Cambridge University Press, 2002)

96   Sheila McLean, *Assisted Dying: Reflections on the Need for Law Reform* (London: Routledge-Cavendish, 2007)

97   Peter Singer, *Rethinking Life and Death: The Collapse of Our Traditional Ethics* (New York: St Martin's Press, 1994)

98   Mary Warnock and Elisabeth Macdonald, *Easeful Death: Is There a Case for Assisted Dying?* (Oxford: Oxford University Press, 2009)

99   Helen Watt, *Life and Death in Healthcare Ethics: A Short Introduction* (London: Routledge, 2000)

100 Simon Woods, *Death's Dominion: Ethics at the End of Life* (Maidenhead, Berkshire: Open University Press, 2007)

Reference bibliography

Academy of Medical Royal Colleges (2008). *A Code of Practice for the Diagnosis and Confirmation of Death* (London: Academy of Medical Royal Colleges).

Airedale NHS Trust v. Bland [1993] 2 WLR 316.

Anon. (2009). '"Dr Death" brings first suicide workshop to UK', *The Daily Telegraph*, 5 May 2009.

Aristotle (2009). *Nicomachean Ethics* [350 BCE], trans. D. Ross and ed. L. Brown (Oxford: Oxford University Press).

BBC News (2002). http://news.bbc.co.uk/onthisday/hi/dates/stories/march/22/newsid_2543000/2543739.stm.

Beauchamp, T.L. and Childress, J.F. (2009). *Principles of Biomedical Ethics*, 6th edn (Oxford: Oxford University Press).

Benjamin, M. (1990). *Splitting the Difference: Compromise and Integrity in Ethics and Politics* (Lawrence, Kansas: University Press of Kansas).

Berlin, I. (1968). *Four Essays on Liberty* (Oxford: Oxford University Press).

Boseley, S. (2002). 'Law decided fate of Mary and Jodie', *The Guardian*, 5 February 2002.

Boseley, S. (2012). 'Tony Nicklinson: Fight to die with dignity "will not be forgotten"', *The Guardian*, 22 August 2012.

Boyle, R.J., Salter, R. and Arnander, M.W. (2004). 'Ethics of refusing parental request to withhold or withdraw treatment from their premature baby', *Journal of Medical Ethics* 30: 402–5.

Brazier, M. (1996). 'Euthanasia and the law', *British Medical Bulletin* 52(2): 317–25.

Bruno, M.A., Vanhaudenhuyse, A., Thibaut, A., Moonen, G. and Laureys, S. (2011). 'From unresponsive wakefulness to minimally conscious

PLUS and functional locked-in syndromes: Recent advances in our understanding of disorders of consciousness', *Journal of Neurology* 258(7):1373–84.

Campbell, A.V. (1998). 'Euthanasia and the principle of justice', in R. Gill (ed.) *Euthanasia and the Churches* (London: Cassell), pp. 83–97.

Campbell, A.V. [forthcoming]. 'Why the body matters: Reflections on John Harris's account of organ procurement', in S. Holm and T. Takala (eds), *A Life of Value* (Amsterdam: Rodopi).

Carroll, L. (1982). *The Complete Illustrated Works of Lewis Carroll* (London: Chancellor Press).

Clark, B. (1984). *Whose Life Is It Anyway? A Full-length Play* (Chicago: Dramatic Publishing Co.).

Clauss, R., and Nel, W. (2006). 'Drug-induced arousal from the permanent vegetative state', *NeuroRehabilitation* 21: 23–8.

Coggon, J. (2007). 'Varied and principled understandings of autonomy in English law: Justifiable inconsistency or blinkered moralism?', *Health Care Analysis* 15: 235–55.

Cohen-Almagor, R. (2004). *Euthanasia in the Netherlands: The Policy and Practice of Mercy Killing* (Dortrecht: Kluwer Academic Publishers).

Commission on Assisted Dying (2012). *'The current legal status of assisted dying is inadequate and incoherent...'* (London: Demos).

Cuttini, M., Rebgliato, M., Bortilo, P. and Hansen, G. (1999). 'Parental visiting, communication, and participation in ethical decisions: a comparison of neonatal unit policies in Europe', *Archives of Disease in Childhood: Fetal & Neonatal* 81: 84–91.

Damasio, A. (1995). *Descartes' Error: Emotion, Reason and the Human Brain* (Sittingbourne, Kent: Quill).

Davis, A. (1998). *Euthanasia: Questions and Answers* (London: Society for the Protection of Unborn Children Handicap Division).

Degrazia, D. (1995). 'Value theory and the best interests standard', *Bioethics* 9: 50–61.

De Haan, J. (2002). 'The ethics of euthanasia: Advocates' perspectives', *Bioethics* 16(2): 154–72.

Director of Public Prosecutions (2010). *Policy for Prosecutors in Respect of Cases of Encouraging or Assisting Suicide* (London: Crown Prosecution Service).

Doyal, L. (2006). 'Dignity in dying should include the legalisation of non-voluntary euthanasia', *Clinical Ethics* 1: 65–7.

Dreger, A.D. (2004). *One of Us: Conjoined Twins and the Future of Normal* (Cambridge, MA: Harvard University Press).

Dworkin, G. (1988). *The Theory and Practice of Autonomy* (Cambridge: Cambridge University Press).

Dworkin, R. (1993). *Life's Dominion: An Argument about Abortion and Euthanasia* (London: HarperCollins).

Fagerlin, A. and Schneider, C.E. (2004). 'Enough: The failure of the living will', *Hastings Center Report* 34(2): 30–42.

Fforde, J. (2001). *The Eyre Affair* (London: Hodder).

Fisher, I. (2006). 'Euthanasia advocate in Italy dies', *New York Times*, 21 December 2006.

Forbes, K. (1998). 'Response to euthanasia and the principle of justice', in R. Gill (ed.), *Euthanasia and the Churches* (London: Cassell), pp. 98–103.

Forbes, K. and Huxtable, R. (2006). 'Editorial: Clarifying the data on double effect', *Palliative Medicine* 20(4): 395–6.

Frankfurt, H.G. (1971). 'Freedom of the will and the concept of a person', *Journal of Philosophy* 68(1): 5–20.

Garcia Márquez, G. (1996). *Of Love and Other Demons* (Harmondsworth: Penguin).

General Medical Council (2013). http://www.gmc-uk.org/guidance/good_medical_practice.asp

George, R. and Regnard, C. (2007). 'Lethal opioids or dangerous prescribers?', *Palliative Medicine* 21: 77–80.

Gillon, R. (1986). 'Suicide and voluntary euthanasia: historical perspective', in P. Downing and B. Smoker (eds), *Voluntary Euthanasia: Experts Debate the Right to Die* (London: Peter Owen), pp. 210–29.

Gillon, R. (1997). '"Futility" – Too ambiguous and pejorative a term?', *Journal of Medical Ethics* 23: 339–40.

Gillon, R. (2003). 'Ethics needs principles – four can encompass the rest – and respect for autonomy should be "first among equals"', *Journal of Medical Ethics 29(5): 307–12.*

Gormally, L. (ed.) (1994), *Euthanasia, Clinical Practice and the Law* (Oxford: The Linacre Centre for Health Care Ethics).

Hagelin, J., Nilstun, T., Hau, J. and Carlsson, H.-E. (2004). 'Surveys on attitudes towards legalisation of euthanasia: importance of question phrasing', *Journal of Medical Ethics* 30: 521–3.

Halliday, R. (1997). 'Medical futility and the social context', *Journal of Medical Ethics* 23: 148–53.

Hanks, G. W. and Twycross, R.G. (1984). 'Letter: Pain, the physiological antagonist of opioid analgesics', *The Lancet*, 30 June: 1477–8.

Harris, J. (1985). *The Value of Life: An Introduction to Medical Ethics* (London: Routledge and Kegan Paul).

Harris, J. (1997). 'The philosophical case against the philosophical case against euthanasia', in J. Keown (ed.), *Euthanasia Examined: Ethical, Clinical and Legal Perspectives* (Cambridge: Cambridge University Press), pp. 36–45.

Harris, D. and Willoughby, H. (2009). 'Resuscitation on television: Realistic or ridiculous? A quantitative observational analysis of the portrayal of cardiopulmonary resuscitation in television medical drama', *Resuscitation* 80: 1275–9.

HE v A Hospital NHS Trust [2003] 2 FLR 408.

Hohfeld, W.N. (1964). *Fundamental Legal Conceptions as Applied in Judicial Reasoning*, ed. W.W. Cook (New Haven and London: Yale University Press).

Homer (2006). *Iliad,* trans. by S. Butler (www.lulu.com).

Homer (2009). *Odyssey,* trans. by S. Butler (www.digireads.com).

Hope, T. (2000). 'Acts and Omissions Revisited', *Journal of Medical Ethics* 26: 227–8.

Reference bibliography

Horn, R.J. (2012). 'Advance directives in England and France: Different concepts, different values, different societies', *Health Care Analysis*.

House of Lords Select Committee (2005). *Assisted Dying for the Terminally Ill Bill [HL]*, Volume I – Report (2005, HL Paper 86-I, Her Majesty's Stationery Office).

Huxtable, R. (2002). '*Re B* (Consent to Treatment: Capacity): A right to die or is it right to die?', *Child and Family Law Quarterly* 14(3): 341–55.

Huxtable, R. (2007). *Euthanasia, Ethics and the Law: From Conflict to Compromise* (London: Routledge-Cavendish).

Huxtable, R. (2009). 'The suicide tourist trap: compromise across boundaries', *Journal of Bioethical Inquiry* 6(3): 327–36.

Huxtable, R. (2012). *Law, Ethics and Compromise at the Limits of Life: To Treat or Not to Treat?* (London: Routledge).

Huxtable, R. and Möller, M. (2007). '"Setting a principled boundary"? Euthanasia as a response to "life fatigue"', *Bioethics* 21(3): 117–26.

Huxtable, R. and Woodley, J. (2005). 'Gaining face or losing face? Framing the debate on face transplants', *Bioethics* 19(5–6): 505–22.

In re Quinlan (1976) NJ 355 A 2d 647.

Jox, R.J. (2011). 'End-of-life decision making concerning patients with disorders of consciousness', *Res Cogitans* 8: 43–61.

Kamisar, Y. (1958). 'Some non-religious views against proposed "mercy killing" legislation', *Minnesota Law Review* 1958; 42(6): 969–1042.

Kant, I. (1991). *The Moral Law: Groundwork of the Metaphysic of Morals*, [1785] trans. and analysed by H.J. Paton (London: Hutchinson and Co.).

Keown, J. (1997). 'Euthanasia in the Netherlands: sliding down the slippery slope?', in J. Keown (ed.), *Euthanasia Examined: Ethical, Clinical and Legal Perspectives* (Cambridge: Cambridge University Press), pp. 261–96.

Keown, J. (2002). *Euthanasia, Ethics and Public Policy: An Argument against Legalisation* (Cambridge: Cambridge University Press).

Kuhse, H. and Singer, P. (1985). *Should the Baby Live? The Problem of Handicapped Infants* (Oxford: Oxford University Press).

Kundera, M. (1999). *The Unbearable Lightness of Being: A Novel* [1984] (London: First Perennial Classic Edition, HarperCollins).

Kutner, L. (1969). 'The Living Will: a proposal', *Indiana Law Journal* 44(1): 539–54.

Laurance, J. (2002). 'Miss B: A woman with much to offer but no desire to live', *The Independent*, 23 March 2002.

Laureys, S., et al. and the European Task Force on Disorders of Consciousness (2010). 'Unresponsive wakefulness syndrome: A new name for the vegetative state or apallic syndrome', *BMC Medicine* 2010: 68.

Luchetti, M. (2010). 'Eluana Englaro, chronicle of a death foretold: Ethical considerations on the recent right-to-die case in Italy', *Journal of Medical Ethics* 36: 333–5.

Mackenzie, C., and Stoljar, N. (eds) (2000). *Relational Autonomy: Feminist Perspectives on Autonomy, Agency, and the Social Self* (Oxford: Oxford University Press).

Magnusson, R.S. (2002). *Angels of Death: Exploring the Euthanasia Underground* (New Haven, CT: Yale University Press).

Malette v Shulman (1987) 47 DLR (4th) 18 (Ontario High Court of Justice).

Malette v Shulman et al. (1990) 72 OR (2d) 417.

Manninen, B. A. (2006). 'A case for justified non-voluntary active euthanasia: exploring the ethics of the Groningen Protocol', *Journal of Medical Ethics* 32: 643–51.

McCall Smith, A. (1999). 'Euthanasia: the strengths of the middle ground', *Medical Law Review* 7: 194–207.

McCarthy, J. (2003). 'Principlism or narrative ethics: must we choose between them?', *Journal of Medical Ethics* 29: 65–71.

McHaffie, H.E., Laing, I.A., Parker, M. and McMillan, J. (2001). 'Deciding for imperilled newborns: medical authority or parental autonomy?' *Journal of Medical Ethics* 27: 104–9.

Monti, M.M., Vanhaudenhuyse, A., Coleman, M.R., Boly, M., Pickard, J.D., Tshibanda, L., Owen, A.M. and Laureys, S. (2010). 'Wilful modulation of brain activity in disorders of consciousness', *New England Journal of Medicine* 362: 579–89.

Morgan, D. (1994). 'Odysseus and the binding directive: nly a cautionary tale?', *Legal Studies* 14(3): 411–42.

Multi-Society Task Force on PVS (1994). 'Medical aspects of the persistent vegetative state', Parts I and II, *New England Journal of Medicine* 330: 1499–1508, 1572–9.

National Health and Medical Research Council (2004). 'Post-coma unresponsiveness (vegetative state): A clinical framework for diagnosis: An information paper' (Canberra, ACT: National Health and Medical Research Council).

NHS Trust v I [2003] EWHC 2243.

Nuffield Council on Bioethics (2006). *Critical Care Decisions in Fetal and Neonatal Medicine: Ethical Issues* (London: Nuffield Council on Bioethics).

Obama, B. (2009). Quoted in http://peacefulparadox.hubpages.com/hub/president-obama-says-living-will-good-idea

Office of Public Prosecutions v Chabot Nederlandse Jurisprudentie (1994) No. 656.

Owen, A.M., Coleman, M.R., Boly, M., Davis, M.H., Laureys, S. and Pickard, J. D. (2006). 'Detecting awareness in the vegetative state', *Science* 313: 1402.

Polack, C. (2001). 'Is a tattoo the answer?' *British Medical Journal* 323: 1063.

Porter, R. (2003). *Flesh in the Age of Reason* (London: Penguin (Allen Lane)).

Prainsack, B. and Buyx, A. (2011). *Solidarity: Reflections on an Emerging Concept in Bioethics* (London: Nuffield Council on Bioethics).

R (on the application of Burke) v General Medical Council [2005] 3 WLR 1132.

Rachels, J. (1997). 'Euthanasia, killing, and letting die', in J. Ladd (ed.), *Ethical Issues Relating to Life and Death* (Oxford: Oxford University Press), pp. 146–63.

Ramsey, J.H.R. (1994). 'A King, a doctor, and a convenient death', *British Medical Journal* 308: 1445.

Re A (Children) (Conjoined Twins: Medical Treatment) [2000] 4 All ER 961.

Re B (Adult: Refusal of Medical Treatment) [2002] 2 All ER 449.

Reid, C., Gooberman-Hill, R. and Hanks, G. (2008). 'Opioid analgesics for cancer pain: symptom control for the living or comfort for the dying? A qualitative study to investigate the factors influencing the decision to accept morphine for pain caused by cancer', *Annals of Oncology* 19: 44–8.

Rietjens, J.A., van der Maas, P.J., Onwuteaka-Philipsen, B.D., van Delden, J.J. and van der Heide, A. (2009). 'Two decades of research on euthanasia from the Netherlands. What have we learnt and what questions remain?' *Journal of Bioethical Inquiry* 6(3): 271–83.

Royal College of Paediatrics and Child Health (2004). *Withholding or Withdrawing Life Saving Treatment in Children: A Framework for Practice*, 2nd edn (London: Royal College of Paediatrics and Child Health).

Royal College of Physicians (2003). *Vegetative State: Guidance on Diagnosis and Management* (London: Royal College of Physicians).

Saunders, C. (1995). 'In Britain: fewer conflicts of conscience', *Hastings Center Report* 25(3): 44–5.

Seale, C. (2006). 'National survey of end-of-life decisions made by UK medical practitioners', *Palliative Medicine* 20(1): 3–10.

Singer, P. (1993). *Practical Ethics*, 2nd edn (Cambridge: Cambridge University Press).

Singer, P. (1994). *Rethinking Life and Death: The Collapse of Our Traditional Ethics* (New York: St Martin's Press).

Smith, S.W. (2005). 'Fallacies of the logical slippery slope in the debate on physician-assisted suicide and euthanasia', *Medical Law Review* 13(2): 224–43.

Smith, T.V. (1942). 'Compromise: its context and limits', *Ethics* 53(1): 1–13.

State of Qld v Alyssa Nolan & Anor [2001] QSC 174.

Sterne, L. (2003). *The Life and Opinions of Tristram Shandy, Gentleman [1759–67]* (Harmondsworth: Penguin Classics).

Sykes, N. and Thorns, A. (2003). 'The use of opioids and sedatives at the end of life', *The Lancet Oncology* 4: 312–18.

Thomas, D. (2000). *Selected Poems* (London: Phoenix).

Thompson, T., Barbour, R. and Schwartz, L. (2003). 'Adherence to advance directives in critical care decision making: Vignette study', *British Medical Journal* 327: 1011–14.

Thomson, J.J. (1971). 'A defense of abortion', *Philosophy & Public Affairs* 1(1): 47–66.

Van Zyl, L. (2000). *Death and Compassion: A Virtue-based Approach to Euthanasia* (Aldershot: Ashgate).

Velleman, J.D. (1992). 'Against the right to die', *Journal of Medicine and Philosophy 17(6): 665–81.*

W v M and S and A NHS Primary Care Trust [2011] EWHC 2443.

Warne-Smith, D. (2007). 'Time capsule: Euthanasia pioneer', *The Australian*, 22 September 2007.

Warnock, M. (ed.) (1962). *Utilitarianism, On Liberty, Essay on Bentham (by John Stuart Mill), together with selected writings of Jeremy Bentham and John Austin* (London: Collins, The Fontana Library).

Weaver, M. (2009). 'Right-to-die teenager Hannah Jones changes mind about heart transplant', *The Guardian*, 21 July 2009.

WHO (2013). http://www.who.int/cancer/palliative/definition/en/

Index

ALL THAT MATTERS: EUTHANASIA

ALL THAT MATTERS: EUTHANASIA

Acknowledgements

The author thanks everyone who read – and commented so helpfully on – all or part of the manuscript: Giles Birchley, Heather Brant, Alastair Campbell, Karen Forbes, Kerry Gutridge, Ruth Horn, Katja Kuehlmeyer, Colette Reid and, in particular, Leighton Huxtable, Lynette Hibbert and Genevieve Liveley.

The author and publisher give their thanks for permission to reproduce the following images and quotations:

Chapter 2 Jodie and Mary © Julia Quenzler **Chapter 3** Ms B © Julia Quenzler **Chapter 4** Odysseus tied to the mast © Leemage/Getty Images **Chapter 6** Charlotte Wyatt © Rex Features **Chapter 7** John Bodkin Adams © Hulton Archive/Getty Images **Chapter 8** Deliverance Machine © Richard Huxtable **Chapter 9** Ciceley Saunders © Ciceley Saunders Institute **Chapter 10** Snakes and Ladders *Artwork:* © Alex Coull *Photograph:* © Richard Huxtable

Chapter 9 Dylan Thomas quotation, taken from *Dylan Thomas: Collected Poems, 1934–1953* (Phoenix, 2003)